MINDFULNESS
THE JOURNEY

Not the Destination

To

Dorene

Enjoy the Journey!

Eleanor Gibson

Love

Eleanor x

**Grosvenor House
Publishing Limited**

This book is published by
Grosvenor House Publishing Ltd
Link House
140 The Broadway, Tolworth, Surrey, KT6 7HT.
www.grosvenorhousepublishing.co.uk

A CIP record for this book
is available from the British Library

Paperback ISBN 978-1-80381-055-3
Hardback ISBN 978-1-80381-188-8
eBook ISBN 978-1-80381-189-5

Contents

Preface

Mindfulness the Journey, Not the Destination is more than a self-help book. It is an amazing journey of self-discovery, understanding and knowledge that brings clarity and motivation into every aspect of our lives.

This book transpired after I was faced with severe trauma in my personal life which led me into a dark, lonely place where I struggled to find a way forward. Through a mindfulness journey, I was able to rebuild a path to a much healthier, worthwhile and fulfilling life. In this book, I will take you on my own personal journey. Through self-analysis, reflection, self-help, poetry and literature I will encourage you to become the driver of your own life, based on mindfulness, compassion and gratitude. By working towards keeping your own mind healthy, you will be helping every other precious life you encounter along the way. By nurturing yourself and focusing on self-care and self-respect, you can find a way of making life easier, simpler and more enjoyable.

No matter what suffering you are experiencing in life, you can find that inner strength to make the situation more bearable. You can start right now, in this moment, to choose the route to a much healthier, meaningful and purposeful life. There is no destination! There is only this moment in time to live, breathe, laugh, cry and dance. It's an ongoing journey and this book, *Mindfulness the Journey, Not the Destination*, is the place to start.

Dedication

I would like to dedicate this book to my beautiful Aunt May, who sadly took her own life on Christmas Eve, 24th December 1960, at the age of 39.

Dear Aunt May,

Sadly, I never had the privilege of getting to know you, or to share my life with you, but through my own troubled journey through life, I truly understand you. Please know that I think about you often and that there will always be a place for you in my heart.

With my deepest sympathy, empathy, love and compassion.

Eleanor xx

Introduction

Lost Not Found

Who am I that lives and breathes
Upon this planet, ill at ease.
With Fate before me in whose hand
I lay my life, misunderstand
The path meandering all around
Which I am on – lost not found.

Found: all of life's great complications.
Lost: all my greatest expectations.
Lost love, lost hope, lost happiness
Found anger, rage, resentfulness.
The tears, the fears and cries of woe
That echo far on distant shore.

Lost I stand alone and fearing
Of the next life now appearing
In the distance grey and sombre
In the deepest darkest yonder.
An island floating out to sea
Awash with sadness, picture me.

by the author

If you can relate to this poem, then this book is for you! The contents of this publication aim to guide you from this state of abyss to a healthier and more positive you! We all need a little help in life sometimes when things get tough. I have used my own life experiences and studies in mindfulness to help me find a clearer way forward in my life. Through self-analysis, reflection, self-help, mindfulness, poetry and literature, I found a coping strategy that works for me. The activities at the end of each chapter can be completed sequentially, as they relate to the chapter contents. However, the mindfulness practices numbered Activity 1, 2, 6, 37 and 38 can be practised at anytime.

I discovered that by compartmentalising my life, I could then begin to understand why I had come to find myself in certain situations. By visiting all the chapters of my life, so far, and writing down my life's story, I was then able to interpret what thought patterns and repetitive actions I had made which were healthy and what routes I had taken that were totally unhealthy and unwise. I realised that by nurturing myself and focusing on self-care and self-respect, I could find a way of making life easier, simpler and more enjoyable. It was like going from rocky road to the freeway and having my own satellite navigation system to guide me on my journey.

No matter what suffering we are experiencing in life, we can find that inner strength to make the situation more bearable. We can start right now, in this moment, to choose the route to a much healthier, meaningful and purposeful life.

There is no destination! There is only this moment in time for us to live, breathe, laugh, cry and dance. It's an ongoing journey and this is the first lesson we learn through mindfulness. We also realise that the road is not going to be a smooth one and, therefore, we need to build up extra reserves through self-care and nurturing so that when we encounter obstacles along the road, we will still find a way forward.

'The best way out is always through.' (Frost, 1914)

Chapter 1

Mindfulness - Waking Up to the Here and Now

The Wandering Mind

'Mindfulness is the opposite of distraction... When the mind becomes tranquil it automatically becomes clearer: like still water, the sediment settles.' (Nairn, 2001, p. 14/15)

It is impossible to think straight if your mind is darting all over the place like balls on a pinball machine. When our mind is in turmoil, we are unable to focus clearly or to be objective and, therefore, we are prone to make decisions and take actions which are not necessarily in our best interests. Mindfulness has helped me to make sense of it all. Instead of my mind being constantly on top spin of the washing machine setting, I can find that inner peace to deal with life's problems.

'Maintaining presence of mind to handle problems calmly and efficiently is a skill that grows with meditation practice.' (Germer, 2009, p.52)

When I started to practise mindfulness, I realised that my mind would wander constantly. I learned, through my studies in mindfulness, that this is perfectly normal, as mindfulness is not about trying to make the mind go blank, but recognising where your mind has wandered to, i.e., what are your thoughts?

Recognising Thinking

Through time, I began to realise that many of my thoughts were negative. I began to see that I was holding on to grudges and fretting about things that had happened in the past and reliving them over and over in my mind. Not only did I discover that negative thoughts would appear, but that I was, in fact, adding extra negativity to the thoughts. This resulted in extra baggage being added to these past experiences. According to the neuroscientist, Rick Hanson, *'Your brain is Velcro for negative experiences and Teflon for positive ones.'* (Cited by Wax, 2018, p.32)

Labelling Thoughts

Labelling these thoughts, when they occurred, during my mindfulness practise, helped me to accept them for what they really were, just thoughts, instead of becoming them.

'Labelling emotions calms the brain.' (Germer, 2009, p.72)

So instead of becoming my thoughts and turning myself into the Incredible Hulk with rage and anger, I could simply name them and let them pass like clouds floating across the sky. Naming my thoughts during mindfulness practise helped me to create a different relationship with them.

'... As we become mindful of our thoughts, we begin to notice a little distance opening up between our thoughts and the mind that is aware of those thoughts.' (Tsoknyi Rinpoche and Swanson, 2012, p.174)

I then began to label my thoughts, such as: disappointment, frustration, despair, anger, sadness, embarrassment, etc. Therefore, when a thought about the time my boss told me I was going to receive a redundancy package and then not being able to follow this through, I don't then become involved in the storyline about how unfair all this was, how let down I was, how misled I was etc., etc. The thought merely becomes one word, i.e., DISAPPOINTMENT.

The day I took a dog on a rope, gifted to me by a classmate, to my Aunt Mary's house, thinking she would be delighted and realising when we went to return it, that the dog actually belonged to someone else. This was HUMILIATION.

The time I was late for an interview in Glasgow due to a traffic jam on the motorway and didn't have time to put money in the parking meter, only to receive a parking ticket. I don't go over the same story, thinking about the "what ifs". What if I had only taken an alternative route? What if I had left earlier? What if I had just gone by train? The memory becomes one word, i.e., FRUSTRATION.

The visit to the supermarket when I requested cash back and the puzzled expression on the sales assistant's face before she said that this was not possible. When I asked her why, she replied, 'Because you paid by cash, not card.' This was STRESS.

The day I was driving to Burnley for a course and missed my turn-off because I was singing along to Boyzone in the car. This can be labelled DISTRACTION.

The night my beloved 20-year-old cat, Spice, died. Realising I would not see her beautiful face and be able to talk to her, clap her or pick her up and cuddle her ever again. This really is SADNESS.

The time my husband took a wrong turning into a field in France, driving into a ditch and subsequently reversing into hidden rocks in the long grass. Instead of asking why he could be so stupid, why he did not stop at the side of the road and check the map, why he continued reversing when the reverse warning signal sounded in the car, I can summarise the story into one word, i.e., DESPAIR.

The time I tried to spend my book vouchers in a book retailer and was told that I couldn't use the voucher towards the purchase of a bookmark. *Really?* No wonder I lost the place! Returning home and writing to the head office of the retail establishment and typing "Dear Sir/Madman" in error, due to my enhanced mental state. This story then doesn't become an epic if you condense it into one word, i.e., ANGER.

The day I tried to return some videos to a shop and was told that I hadn't hired the videos in the first place, but had actually bought them. Instead of beating myself up for not realising that the hire videos were at the other side of the shop and that I should have realised this by the price, and recalling the smirk on the faces of all the other customers and the sales assistant, I recognised this as EMBARRASSMENT.

Alive and Breathing

Before I found mindfulness, my mind was so stressed that I didn't realise that, in this present moment, I could pause and look at the beautiful sky, the puffy white clouds, I could hear birds chirping, smell flowers, enjoy a cup of tea and feel the earth beneath my feet. I didn't realise that I was indeed *alive and breathing*. How wonderful!

'The simple act of sitting in a stable upright posture with calmness and dignity has an importance all its own.' (Rosenberg and Guy, 2004)

The breath is so important as,

> *'The simple vehicle of the breath takes the practitioner from calming the mind all the way to the deepest wisdom, to nirvana.'* (Rosenberg and Guy, 1998, p.3)

I am alive! You are alive! How good is this?

> *'... As long as you are breathing, there is more right with you than wrong with you.'* (Kabat-Zinn, 2013, p.xlix)

Activity 1 – Labelling Thoughts

- Find a quiet place to sit, making sure that you are comfortable
- Adopt a dignified posture (sitting in an upright position either on a chair with feet flat on the floor or sitting on a meditation cushion with the back straight. Hands resting on the thighs – either with palms facing upwards or downwards. Or alternatively, one hand placed on top of the other with palms facing upwards and thumbs gently touching.)
- Be aware of the ground beneath the body and the space surrounding the body
- Now focus on your breathing
- Perhaps breathing a little more deeply than normal
- Be totally aware of the breath as it enters the body and totally aware of the breath as it leaves the body
- Try to make the in breath the same length as the out breath
- Breath after breath
- So just being with the gentle rhythm of the breath
- As you sit here breathing, you may discover that the mind has wandered off
- Simply recognise where it has wandered to
- Label the thought using one word
- Imagine placing the word on a leaf and gently placing the leaf on a gently flowing stream
- Letting the leaf float downstream and disappear from view

- Return your focus to the breathing
- Each time a thought occurs, label it and place it on a leaf, letting it float away down stream
- Continue this meditation practise for a few minutes
- Now return to the body breathing and let your breathing return to its natural rhythm
- Be aware of the stability of the ground beneath the body and the space surrounding the body
- Gently place your right hand over the heart area and gently say:

    May I be happy, may I be healthy, may I live in peace
    May others be happy, may they be healthy, may they live in peace

    Now take a moment to be grateful for this precious moment in time.

Activity 2 – The Present Moment – Awakening the Senses

Sit down. Take up a dignified posture. Be aware of your body breathing. Be totally aware of the breath as it enters the body and totally aware of the breath as it leaves the body. Just be with the gentle rhythm of your breathing in this moment. See if you can make the in breath the same length as the out breath. Just focus on the breathing for the next few moments being aware of how soothing the rhythm of your breath can be. Now letting go of the focus on the breath, tune into what is happening in the present moment:

- **What can you see?**
- **What can you hear?**
- **Be totally aware of your sense of smell. What aromas are presenting themselves to you?**

- **What can you taste in this moment? Is your mouth dry or moist?**
- **What textures and surfaces can you feel in this present moment?**
- **What temperature are you experiencing in this moment?**
- **Just sit still for a few moments and fully experience this precious moment in time.**

This simple mindfulness activity opens up our world to the here and now. We are able to pause and totally experience what is happening.

I realised, through my mindfulness practise, that I had become detached from the world. Mindfulness awakened my senses and made me feel alive again! I discovered that, somehow, I had become disconnected from the world around me, feeling as if I did not belong. This took me on a journey to discover who I actually was. I realised that I had somehow managed to lose myself along the way and mindfulness led me on this wonderful journey of self-discovery. I needed to know my own mind.

'Knowing your mind not only leads to a happy life, it transforms every trace of confusion and wakes us up completely.' (Dzogchen Ponlop Rinpoche, 2011, p.31)

I asked myself the same question over and over. *Who am I?* The only way I could make sense of it all was to start at the very beginning.

Chapter 2

The Journey through
Life – Childhood

The Journey Begins

To be able to enjoy childhood should be every child's right. To see each day as a new beginning, an adventure full of wonder and awe was what my childhood was all about.

I was born in 1960, in Motherwell, an industrial town, in the west of Scotland. I was the middle child of three. My older sister, June, was six years older and my younger sister, Moira, was two years younger.

Childhood Memories

The first memories that I can recall are of my Uncle Alex's beautiful garden at Cumbrae Drive, Motherwell, with its pristine roses, gorgeous gladioli and marigolds. In his back garden, he had a carpet beater pole which we used to

swing from and burl around. I remember the little flowerbeds at the back door which had shell-decorated borders. In his garden hut, there were always onions or spring onions hanging to dry and we used to joke that we were going to buy him a bicycle, beret and stripy top so that he could sell his produce. He also grew strawberries, beetroot, rhubarb and kale. Two doors along from my uncle's house lived a lovely Welsh lady with a kind heart and a love for people. Her warmth, compassion and zest for life remains with me to this day. In her company, the world always seemed bright, happy and safe.

Mum, Dad, my two sisters and I lived in a newly built housing complex, called McClurg Court, situated at the other end of the town. It was a flat-roofed building in the beginning but someone, somewhere, realised that flat roofs are not ideal in Scotland due to the amount of rain, snow and frost. The council eventually added an appropriately designed peaked roof.

The building itself was, otherwise, well designed for families. We had a balcony off the living room and a balcony off the larger bedroom. To access our home, we used a communal landing which we all had to maintain the cleanliness of, as well as the close area. At nine years old, I remember having to wash down the close and landing with the help of my two sisters, as it was our "turn".

The base of the building consisted of pensioner flats, small and compact with a tiny lounge, bedroom, kitchen and bathroom with a half-sized bath. The next floor, where we lived, had two storeys and these residences were termed as maisonettes. We had two bedrooms, whereas the accommodation at the sides of the building were designed to house larger families and consisted of three bedrooms and were all on the one level.

The building was abuzz with young families. At the rear of the property, we had pram shelters but no one dared keep a pram in them as they were damp, fusty and crawling with spiders and woodlice. These outbuildings also contained the bin shelters, which were always overflowing and pungent with rotten debris.

We had communal drying greens where we used to hang out our washing on a sort of informal rota basis. These drying greens were also where we played pole tig. There was always the sound of children playing hide and seek, chap-door-run-fast, or playing at peever, skipping ropes and elastic ropes. I realised, however, that no one seemed interested in playing skipping ropes with me after my tooth brace fell to the ground with a clatter whilst I was skipping. As it appeared to be an alien object, which had appeared from nowhere, everyone screamed and ran indoors, leaving me feeling somewhat lonely, rejected and abandoned. This left me with a bit of a complex, but I was never really good at skipping anyway.

On rainy days, we held concerts in the middle close area. Again, everyone seemed to head indoors when I got the opportunity to sing, but, hey, we couldn't all be the Neil Reids or Lena Zavaronis of our day. Rainy days were also good days for playing ball in the close and my younger sister, Moira, was excellent at this. All she needed were two rubber balls or tennis balls. Her favourite rhyme to accompany her juggling skills was as follows:

'A house to let
Apply within
A lady put out
For drinking gin
For gin you know
Is a very bad thing
As I go out and my neighbour comes in.'

The tennis or rubber balls had then to be skilfully caught by the next player. I suppose it was a bit like relay races without the baton.

The ball games really seemed to upset the residents and there were many complaints, as the constant thud of a ball hitting the wall echoed far beyond the close area. This did not deter us from continuing to play this delightful game, even after the "No Ball Games" sign was displayed. Honestly, do grown-ups always feel a compulsion to complain about everything! Where was their *joie de vivre*?

Many of the girls went to "electrocution" lessons on Monday evenings, so after a great deal of nagging and persuasion, I was also allowed to go to elocution lessons, but I really didn't know what it entailed. I stupidly thought that it was along the lines of gymnastics, or something similar. This is where my love of poetry and literature began. Mrs Crosbie was an excellent teacher and I managed to sit and pass every exam grade through the London College of Music, achieving my associateship in 1977. Little did I know that this qualification and associated study of poetry and literature would be so important to my personal life, career and mindfulness teachings.

The elocution lessons also led me to enjoy drama and to take part in performances at the drama festival held by Dalziel High School, annually, at Cleland Estate. My acting skills were recognised by our head teacher, Mr Scobbie, who nominated  me for a scholarship from the Motherwell and Wishaw Round Table to travel to Austria, with the older pupils, to study Mozart and practice my German speaking skills. *Jawohl*!

I always found staying away from my home and my family quite stressful, although my trip to Austria proved to be educational and enjoyable. On my return, I had to give a presentation to the Motherwell and Wishaw Round Table, explaining what I had gained from receiving the scholarship, which was quite a daunting experience for a 14-year-old. I was accompanied by my father, so all was right with the world, as he always instilled in me the confidence to succeed.

I remember going to Kerswell College with the Geography Society and going hillwalking and orienteering with one of our very handsome teachers, Ross Davidson, the PE teacher, who starred in *EastEnders* as Andy, the nurse. He was also a dancer on the television programme called *Thingummyjig*. On this weeklong visit, I experienced quite a number of new things: what powdered scrambled egg tastes like and how your feet feel after walking miles in hiking boots, which are two sizes too big, and how it feels to touch a farmer's fence which has an electric current running through it – OUCH!

I also learned how your imagination can run riot when your schoolmates are telling scary stories about patients escaping from the nearby state hospital in Carstairs with the sole purpose of murdering us in our beds. Imagine the screams when our teacher came to the dorm to check that we were all safely tucked up in our beds for the night. My mother wrote to me and said how much I was missed by the family and that even the budgie was struggling without me. This reduced me to tears but I only cried under the covers at night, for fear of others in the dormitory laughing at me.

Holidays

My family was privileged to have a car and this led us on many journeys to destinations which were new and inspiring. We would spend our summer holidays at faraway places such as Dawlish Warren in Devon, Clacton-on-Sea, Southend-on-Sea, Great Yarmouth, Skegness and Blackpool. I have many fond memories of these vacations which remain with me and have influenced the way that I view the world. It is amazing the things that stick in your mind.

I remember:

- Being on the big wheel at Great Yarmouth, with fantastic views of the entire resort.
- The time we went sailing along the Norfolk Broads and having to moor every ten minutes, as the three greenish bananas I had eaten, in quick succession, were causing havoc with the digestive system.
- The day my younger sister, Moira, adopted a live ladybird as a pet and kept it in a matchbox. This matchbox was left in a cafe and, embarrassingly, the entire family returned to the venue to ask of its whereabouts as Lady, who was now a family member, had gone astray. We were all devastated when the matchbox, and its precious inhabitant, had vanished without trace.
- The time our dad gave us one pound each to spend on the amusement machines and the look on his face when we returned after 15 minutes to say that we had spent all of it.
- The vacation in the converted railway carriages in Dawlish Warren, when we emptied our Pinky and Perky piggy banks to buy something special from the toy shop. The look of sheer frustration and murmurings from my mother for buying two identical books, shaped like grandfather clocks with moving hands, so I could teach my

younger sister how to tell the time, has never left me. (After all, the teacher always has to have her own copy of the book she is teaching from).

- The trip to Devon when we lost my uncle's dog, Sandy, at the motorway service station en route, only to find him under someone's table being fed titbits.
- The time when I won first prize in the talent contest at the caravan site at Clacton-on-Sea, two weeks in succession, for singing badly.
- The three occasions when I got lost on the beach and my name was announced on the loudspeaker to be collected by my demented parents.
- The disgusted look on my mother's face when I approached her with a "worm" on a safety pin, which the lovely couple at the next door caravan gave me to eat out of a shell (whelks were not regarded as a delicacy by my mother!).
- The caravan holiday at Byne Hill in Ayrshire, where I kept falling in the river, as stepping stones required good balance. This always resulted in me having to spend the rest of the day without footwear, as I only had one pair of gutties.
- The day a gypsy approached my father on the beach and asked him to buy some wares. His refusal to buy anything led to an exchange of words, with the gypsy cursing and telling him that he would not see his 52nd birthday. Perhaps it's just coincidence that he died at the age of 51.

Remembering

Memories from my childhood include:

- My first day at primary school, being puzzled by the children around me crying. I didn't find the need to cry but when I turned around to wave to Mum, I discovered that she was crying. I remember being given a small blackboard and told to draw continuous "e"s. We were then instructed by the teacher to draw the opposite, like upside down "e"s. I simply turned my little blackboard around and showed the teacher. She had a look of sheer frustration on her face. I think I realised, very early on, that you can achieve the same outcome with minimum effort by just simply using your initiative. However, it appeared that this was obviously not to be encouraged at Glencairn Primary School.
- My first arithmetic lesson entailed the teacher drawing a house on the main blackboard at the front of the class. She drew a line and illustrated that there were two floors in the house and that the house contained ten people. 'If five people are upstairs, how many are downstairs?' she asked.
- The feeling of delight and pride when Miss Cormack placed my first poem on the classroom wall in primary three:

The Donkey

Once I saw a donkey
Riding by the sea
And oh it was so pretty
Much prettier than me.

- The beautiful summer's day that we sat in the playground, in small groups, and learned how to work a sundial. We had to draw lines on a piece of paper every fifteen minutes to show that the shadow of our homemade sundial had moved. I suggested to my group that we could achieve more lines on our piece of paper if we simply kept moving the dial. On discovering our experiment, the teacher appeared to be having a fit of rage. Honestly, didn't she realise that fifteen minutes is a long time in a child's life to be sitting doing nothing!

- The day my older sister, June, won first prize in a knitting competition and how proud I was of her.

- The time we spent playing on the building site, rolling the drainage pipes with one person inside, whilst the rest of us pushed, and accidently running the concrete pipe over my sister, Moira's finger.
- The time I sat on chewing gum in the Duchess Park, whilst wearing my new pink hot pants, and having to make a heart-shaped patch to cover the damaged material for the rest of the summer, as it was made perfectly clear to me that I wasn't getting a new pair.
- The day I spent with Dad, when he was dying of lung cancer, reading aloud *Cider with Rosie* by Laurie Lee.
- The beautiful sunny afternoon that I jumped in a pile of soot on the waste ground beside our house and my mother washing me in the kitchen sink as my friends sniggered outside the kitchen window.
- The day the whole family went to the opening of the Forth Road Bridge in 1964.
- The morning I opened the pram shelter door, after being on holiday for two weeks, to find that my sister's bike had been stolen.
- The sunny summer evening that my dad bought me a piano for £5 and wheeled it to our house from the next street.
- The day the head teacher at primary school asked me why I hadn't taken my bicycle to be checked by the police for road

worthiness on Saturday morning. To which I boldly replied 'I don't own a bike.'

'Why did you sign up to take part in the cycling proficiency programme, then?' he shouted.

'I didn't know I needed a bike to take part,' I sheepishly replied.

'Are you completely stupid!' he yelled. At this, he stormed out of the classroom. Honestly, grown-ups can be so childish!

- The afternoon my friend, Yvonne, from primary school invited me to her house after school to smoke cigarettes. She lived in the posher, private houses known as Airbles Estate. 'Bring your own cigarettes,' she said. So, for two weeks, I collected cigarette ends from the ashtrays at home and hid them behind the bedroom curtain. At Yvonne's house, I had just, shakily, lit my first cigarette end and was taking my first puff when my sister, Moira, arrived on the scene. Imagine her face when she caught sight of me with the cigarette. My face was also a picture. She ran all the way home to clipe to my parents before I had the opportunity to stop her. That was the first and last time I smoked cigarettes. My sister probably, on hindsight, saved me from becoming a chain-smoker. The shame I felt at the time was quite overwhelming!

- The day my younger sister, Moira, and I, appeared on *Songs of Praise* in 1966, walking from the church into the Sunday school at St. Mary's Parish Church, Motherwell.

- The night my older sister, June, won first prize at a Halloween party for her outstanding costume which she had spent weeks decorating using silver foil milk bottle tops.

- The visits to Johnston's, the paper shop, which was just a stone's throw away from where we lived and had a very distinctive smell of newspapers.

- The times we spent in Chrissie Wilson's wool shop in Windmillhill Street, which was so cluttered that you could hardly move. I know, for sure, that it would not meet any health and safety standards today. Mrs Wilson always appeared to know where everything was though!

- The first time I tasted the best millionaire's shortbread, which my older sister made.
- The occasions when my mother had a twenty-pound club at the Co-operative department store, or big store, as it was known locally. This was used to purchase new outfits at Easter for wearing to Sunday school. This  consisted of a new coat, shoes and hat and sometimes a proper Easter bonnet. The twenty-pound club was also used to purchase school uniforms. The big store was amazing and seemed to sell everything. I was always fascinated by the suction machine at the till which sent the bill and bank notes to the accounts office and, moments later, spat out a tube which enclosed the receipt and change.
- The daily visits to Hendry's, the shop I frequented on my way to school, to buy a packet of plain crisps for 3p and something from the penny tray. I did like value for money! I refrained from buying flavoured crisps, as they were 4p. However, I do remember a period of time when I stopped buying crisps altogether as Mrs Hendry, the shopkeeper, advised that if I continued to eat as many crisps, I would eventually turn into one. 'One morning, your mother will come to wake you up for school and under the blankets all she will find is a giant crisp!' she advised. Really! Do adults realise the effects of the spoken word on a small child with a big imagination?
- The mealtimes when Uncle Alex encouraged us to eat our soup as "it would stick to our ribs". This really perplexed me as the last thing I wanted was to be walking around with carrot, turnip, leek and barley stuck to my body. 'Eat up your crusts,' he would say, 'it will give you curly hair'. Really? Has this

been scientifically proven? This is maybe the reason that I still have to use hair straighteners on a regular basis.

- The days we spent on Ayr Beach, which is beautiful in the sunshine. We idled away the hours paddling, swimming, picnicking and building our dream sandcastles as the sun soothed and healed our bodies. Just listening to the sound of the great outdoors presenting itself to us made us feel totally alive. Water has a therapeutic quality all of its own, bringing a sense of soothing, cleansing and healing.
- The weekend outings to the Mennock Pass and the Dalveen Pass where we set up the picnic rug and enjoyed kite-flying, fishing or paddling in the river and savouring the beautiful outdoors.

Being young was awesome. Each day filled with brand new experiences. Summer brought warmth, excitement and a sense of fulfilment. Sun-kissed days packed with activities that fuelled the imagination. In my youth, children seemed happy and laughter filled the summer days with a warm glow of joy of simply being alive. My childhood was full of adventure – stretching the imagination and providing a platform for growth spiritually, mentally, physically and emotionally. When we did falter or need comfort, there was always someone to show genuine care – perhaps a relative, a teacher, a neighbour or family friend.

In childhood, the sky seemed bluer and brighter, almost like deep water. Friendships blossomed like flowers during the summer months. Sharing the warmth and tranquility of the season invigorated our bodies, minds and souls. After spending the day outdoors, rest, in the form of sleep was such a welcome relief. Night always appeared like a deep, dark blue blanket, with sparkly, glistening stars. The end of each day felt blissful and complete.

This poem captures fond memories of my childhood:

Remember

Remember the glorious days of our youth!
Of summers that glowed,
Of laughter that peeled.
Remember the feeling of
love in our hearts
For life in abundance,
Of hurt when it healed.
Remember the hours we
spent on the beach,
The warmth of the sun,
The seagulls that screech
The lapping of waves
As they pound on the shore
The feeling of peace
When each day was o'er.

Remember the touch of a petal of rose,
The scent of the honeysuckle,
The songs we composed.
The sky with its blueness,
Its brightness so deep,
The love that we shared,
The secrets we keep.

Remember the sun as it fell from the sky,
Into deep depths of darkness
Of seas rising high.
Remember the stars scattered brightly above,
And sleep when it came,
In a blanket of love.

by the author

Activity 3 – Happy Memories of Childhood

- Write down five happy memories from your childhood (e.g. paddling in the sea, flying a kite, playing hide and seek, horse riding, building a sandcastle, playing a sport, completing a jigsaw or playing a board game).
- Close your eyes and bring these memories to life in your mind's eye, one by one. After each delightful memory, open your eyes and write down random words that capture your experience. Be mindfully aware of where you are experiencing these fond memories in the body.
- Write down the sensations you experienced in the body during this exercise.

Activity 4 – Childhood Activities Revisited

- Go back to your list of fond memories. What activities could you still enjoy today? Write these down.
- Re-connect with your inner child and re-live those happy memories by doing the activities again.

(Note: perhaps you went horse riding as a child but feel you could not do that anymore. How could you recapture the enjoyment of this through your senses i.e. seeing, hearing, smelling, touching? Perhaps clapping a horse could regenerate some of that feeling of joy from your childhood).

Activity 5 – Capturing Happy Memories of Childhood

Find a song, poem, photograph or postcard which captures good memories from your childhood.

Activity 6 – Appreciating the Great Outdoors

Visit a park, beach, forest or garden or sit by a river. Take time to look around you as if experiencing the great outdoors for the first time.

Ask yourself:-

- What can I see?
- What can I hear?
- What smells are present?
- What is the temperature?
- How am I feeling? i.e. happy, joyful or sad.
- Where am I experiencing this in the body? i.e. warmth in the head or tummy, heaviness at the heart.

Chapter 3

The Journey through Life – Adolescence

The Teenage Years

Adolescence can be quite stressful, as it is a time in life when we are desperately trying to find ourselves. We really need strong mentors to guide us through and help us to build stable foundations for our adult life, as the world around us can appear to be quite overwhelming.

Being a middle child, with middle child syndrome, actually proved to work in my favour. I was forced to figure many things out for myself, as my parents always seemed to be preoccupied. The pre-teen years were a little bit daunting. Discovering that my parents seemed totally incompatible really complicated and clouded my view of the world, as they perceived everything from an entirely different viewpoint.

In fact, they were complete opposites, both mentally and physically. My mother had black hair and brown eyes and my father had blond hair and blue eyes. My father was hard-working, sensitive, interested in politics and loved poetry. He wanted us to do well at school and if he recognised that we had a particular talent in any educational subject, then he tried his best to encourage this. My mother, on the other hand, was not exactly a workaholic, seemed cold and distant. She certainly had no interest in current affairs or literature. She loved to go out for meals or tea and in the summer months she sunbathed at every opportunity. She did not encourage us academically and would often say to me, 'Put that book away, it will hurt your eyes.' My mother was quite vain and needed to wear glasses but refrained from doing so due to her self-image. I knew that my eyesight was not perfect and always opted, when possible, to sit at the front of the classroom at school so that I could read the blackboard. It was not until I started work that I realised how short-sighted I actually was. My medical examination for my first job flagged up my need to wear glasses.

I think that growing up with parents who have conflicting viewpoints and priorities can confuse children as there is no clear-cut guidance on which direction you should be taking in life. This aspect of confusion has remained with me throughout my adult life.

I recently studied a school class photograph and did not recognise myself – a conscientious pupil who enjoyed life to the full! In your teenage years, I think you are desperately trying to find yourself. Starting secondary school is such a daunting experience for everyone. New beginnings, new friendships, new subjects to learn and discovering that life is maybe a little more complicated than you initially thought.

I was educated at Dalziel High School, Motherwell, where our head teacher, Mr Scobbie, inspired us to follow the school motto, *summa petenda* – "aim for the highest". At Dalziel, I received a first-class education and every pupil was given the opportunity to excel. Each year, we were encouraged to raise funds for the upkeep of Cleland Estate, owned by the school, and I proudly served on the cake and candy stall.

The grounds at Cleland Estate were magnificent and included rugby, football and hockey pitches. We also had a 400-metre running track and I loved to take part in the school sports day with discus throwing, javelin throwing, 100 metres sprint, relay race, high jump and long jump. I used to thoroughly enjoy cross-country running. For the less energetic, there was a well stocked library on the premises. We also had changing facilities and showers. Wednesday afternoons were spent at Cleland Estate and some Saturday mornings to play hockey.

I loved to learn new things and spent a lot of time at my local church, taking part in all sorts of activities. I was a Brownie Guide, Guide and Ranger Guide. Being part of these organisations really helped me by providing social skills, housekeeping skills and a sense of honour and respect. Taking part in the Duke of Edinburgh's

Award scheme taught me many skills, such as flower arranging, public speaking and organisational skills.

The stable foundations built in these organisations have never left me to this day. Fond memories of camping at Netherurd, badge work, such as hostess badge, observers badge and knitting badge, have all added to my life's tapestry.

My childhood years were a blur of activities: Monday – Elocution; Tuesday – Brownies, Guides or Ranger Guides; Wednesday – Swimming at Motherwell baths; Thursday – God Squad; Friday – Piano lessons; Saturday – Hockey, followed by days away in the car; Sunday – Sunday school or Youth Fellowship and horse riding at Dalzell Estate, Motherwell.

I remember, at the age of thirteen, being in love with Donny Osmond. The *Jackie* magazine provided posters of him. The first week enclosed his legs, the next week his torso and the third week his head. I diligently sellotaped the pieces together and proudly displayed these posters on my bedroom wall. At that time, I truly believed that I couldn't possibly be in love with anyone else.

I remember with amusement the strong fashion statements of my teenage years: the feather-cut hairstyle, the tank tops, the bell bottom trousers, American tan tights and platform shoes!

I remember from high school being talked into going to the shops in Brandon Street, Motherwell, at lunchtime (which was totally out of bounds for all pupils) by my friend, Valerie. 'We won't get caught,' she assured me, 'I've been doing it for weeks.' Well, you can easily guess what happened. One of our teachers spotted us in Woolworths and we were reported to the headmaster. I will never forget the feeling of shame and humiliation for breaking the school rules.

When I was fourteen, we went on our first family holiday abroad together to C'an Picafort in Majorca. My mother spent every day sunbathing whilst Dad encouraged us to speak Spanish and learn all about the local cuisine and culture. The flight home was memorable, as my sister, Moira, and I had purchased large, standing, ornamental donkeys, which we had to hold all the way back on the flight.

Feelings

When I was sixteen, I returned to school for 6th year with a heavy heart as most of my friends left school at the end of 5th year. One person in particular left and took my heart with them, leaving me struggling to recover. He was my closest friend and always motivated me to try to achieve higher grades in all my schoolwork, as he was so talented in every subject. In his company, the world was the most amazing place to be and he filled my heart with joy. Losing my soulmate and idol left me feeling devastated. Perhaps I wasn't in love with Donny Osmond after all! The following song expresses my feelings of loss:

Feelings

Nothing more than feelings,
Trying to forget my
Feelings of love…
Teardrops,
Rolling down on my face
Trying to forget my
Feelings of love
Feelings for all my life I'm feeling
I wish I'd never met you _ _ _
You'll never come again' (Albert, 1975)

Activity 7 – Teen Memories that Make You Smile

Write down five amusing things that you can remember from your adolescence.

Activity 8 – Life Skills Learned in Adolescence

Write down five life skills which you learned during your teenage years.

Activity 9 – Songs from Your Teenage Years

Think of songs which remind you of your adolescent years. Try to source these songs and enjoy the lovely memories again.

Activity 10 – Fashion Statements of Your Teenage Years

Write down any fashion items of clothing which were prominent during your teenage years.

Activity 11 – Friendships

Write down names of close friends from your teenage years.
Write down five happy memories that you shared with friends during your teenage years.

Chapter 4

The Journey through Life – Loss of a Loved One

Recalling Happy Memories of a Loved One

Dad was my inspiration, motivation and centre of my universe. He would always encourage me to do my best. 'Reach for the stars and you will get them!' he would enthuse.

He would always support us in taking up new activities and worked hard to provide for the family. He was always helping people by fixing their cars but, unfortunately, they insisted on paying him for their motor repairs by giving him cigarettes, which did, in my opinion, contribute to his poor health.

When Dad was around, I felt confident and all was right with the world. When I practised reciting for my elocution lessons, he was a great critic and wouldn't settle for second best. Everything had to be perfect.

Dad was always busy working at Adams, the butchers, or carrying out maintenance at the Co-operative bakery. However, he

still always managed to find time to take us to places such as Moffat, Peebles, Biggar, Troon, Ayr or the Forth Bridges. At Biggar, we always went for a high tea at the Elphinstone, or the chip shop on the main street.

Dad had a great sense of humour and would wake us up for school in the morning by pretending to play the bugle outside our bedroom door. My younger sister, Moira, was given the nickname of "Tammy Troot". He loved the Flintstones and would greet us with a "yabba dabba doo!" on returning home from work. He loved poetry, especially the work of Robert Burns.

When I was fourteen, my father was diagnosed with lung cancer and we spent two years visiting hospitals and trying to put on a brave face to the rest of the world.

Time

When someone you love is diagnosed with a terminal illness, your world stands still – you enter a parallel universe to the rest of society. Each day seems like a precious gift but also an uphill struggle to hold on to what is left. Just begging for the clock to stop and preserve this withering human being, to hold on to every breath, every morsel of life with a heavy pendulum for a heart.

Time

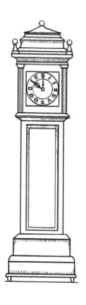

The heavy hands of time stand still
Like the grinding wheels of a watermill
Where drought has starved it of its need
To function smoothly, flow with speed.

Each droplet precious to its aim
To reach its goal and movement gain.
Like Time is holding back reserve
To grasp each moment to preserve.

This perfect setting locked in time
Enchanting feelings, so sublime.
No fear, no sound, the scent of dill
Let heavy hands of time stand still.

by the author

Funeral Blues

I think losing a parent when your own body and mind are hormonally trying to find themselves is emotionally draining. Spending so much time with a dying parent makes you lose your own identity, and their loss of life becomes yours.

When he died, I felt as if my world had come to an abrupt end. I was overwhelmed with grief and felt a huge void had appeared in my life:-

'Funeral Blues

Stop all the clocks, cut off the telephone,
Prevent the dog from barking with a juicy bone,
Silence the pianos and with muffled drum
Bring out the coffin, let the mourners come.

Let aeroplanes circle moaning overhead
Scribbling on the sky the message He Is Dead,
Put crepe bows round the white necks of the public doves,
Let the traffic policemen wear black cotton gloves.

He was my North, my South, my East and West,
My working week and my Sunday rest,
My noon, my midnight, my talk, my song;
I thought that love would last for ever: I was wrong.

The stars are not wanted now: put out every one;
Pack up the moon and dismantle the sun;
Pour away the ocean and sweep up the wood;
For nothing now can ever come to any good.'

(Auden, 1938)

My father's death impacted greatly on our family and left a huge void in all of our lives. My academic path had suddenly changed due to financial circumstances and I found myself having to leave school prematurely in order to find paid employment. My dream of a university education had been extinguished.

Activity 12– Words of Grief

Write down words which express your grief of losing a loved one.

Activity 13 – Feelings of Loss and Grief

Using these words create one verse of poetry or prose which sums up your feelings of loss and grief.

Activity 14 – Feelings of Loss Experienced in the Body

Write down where you experience this sense of loss in the body.

Activity 15 – Songs that Express Your Grief

Find a song or poem which captures your experience of grief.

Activity 16 – Fond Admiration of a Loved One

Write down five things that you admired about your loved one.

Activity 17 – Fond Memories of Your Loved One

Write down five lovely memories you have of your loved one.

Activity 18 – In Touch With Your Feelings of Happy Memories

Close your eyes and revisit these happy experiences, one by one and be mindful of where you experience these precious memories in the body.

Chapter 5

The Journey through Life – Work

Starting Work

So many demands on our time make it difficult for us to give 100% to every part of our lives. If 100% is given to our career prospects, this can have detrimental effects on health, family and home life.

Having a career and family can be challenging. If demands at work are high, then always make provision for family. Ensure that your loved ones are given the best possible care at all times. When you have the opportunity to spend time with your family, make sure that they know that you care and that you are always working in their best interests. If time is in short provision, try and find a mutual pastime which you can share and enjoy together, e.g. board games, badminton, jigsaws, cycling, swimming, walking, football or tennis. This enables you to enjoy and share your downtime together, creating special memories for years to come.

One of my greatest achievements in life has been through my work. In every job I have been employed in, I always did the best I could. In a working environment it is always important to show respect for others, no matter what level we are at in the organisation.

'It's nice to be important but more important to be nice.'
(Cox, 2021)

I think more of this message should be taught as part of continuous professional development in all working environments. My work has never been about ego but about providing the best service possible to the organisation I am employed with, who have been good enough to employ me.

The Work Journey

I started work as an accounts assistant on 22nd November 1976. My heart had been set on becoming a speech therapist but I knew that there was no financial support available for my studies. I found the work interesting and easy, using the Kalamazoo method of wages. Every Friday, Ina, Maureen and I were locked in our office to make up the wage packets. My first pay packet was £20.65.

I was soon promoted to the main accounts office from the wages section, where I managed to impress the accountant by balancing the work in progress ledger at my first attempt! I remember being given the task of collecting the tea and coffee money each week from the office staff and shop floor workers. I was very naive and didn't realise how dishonest people could be. The lengths that some people would go to avoid paying always baffled me. People were known to hide in the toilet until my collecting visit was over. On one occasion, I decided to enter the toilets to collect the outstanding amounts, only to find two women fighting on the floor, so I made a speedy exit. My job also entailed covering tea breaks and carrying out holiday breaks on the switchboard and reception duties. I was also asked to translate telex messages from France and Germany.

I moved from Fabritek to Motherwell Bridge Engineering, accounts section. I was only in the door when redundancy notices were being handed out so I only stayed there for nine months. I didn't enjoy sales ledger work, having to work out retention percentages, etc. The accountant and his assistant also made the job more difficult as frequently they would fall out and I had to act as the go-between. It went something like this. 'Tell Archie I need the final sales figures by noon.'

Archie, who was sitting at the next desk, could hear him asking me to do this. Archie retorted, 'Tell Mr Toft that the report will not be ready until 2pm.'

I then stated, 'Mr Toft, Archie says that the report won't be ready until two.'

Mr Toft, whose face was turning a deep shade of crimson, shouted, 'Tell Archie one o'clock at the latest and he will have to work through the lunch hour!' Archie would then start shouting at me and ask me if I thought he was Superman or something. Not in my wildest dreams could I picture Archie in Lycra or tights! Honestly, don't shoot the messenger! I am sure that the skills acquired in this post would stand me in good stead for running a crèche!

When I started working in the direct works department of Strathclyde Regional Council, I realised that my uncle worked there and rumour then spread that he got me the job. Honestly, that I should need someone like him to get me a telephonist/receptionist job anywhere beggars belief! I was promoted to personnel assistant, a job I truly hated. I was totally unaware that people had so many personal problems and that they struggled to do a day's work. I mean, how hard can it be? Making up disciplinary records all week did not excite or stimulate me. I then got a transfer to the area office in Larkhall and discovered that many more people were suffering from mental health problems in the working environment than I could ever have imagined. Or was it just me?

When I moved to the careers service in the council headquarters building in Almada Street, Hamilton, I worked with a delightful gentleman called Mr Henderson. It was a pleasure going into the office and working with him. He had a lovely personality and wicked sense of humour. He loved to do his impersonation of the "Orange walk" on a regular basis, much to the bewilderment and dismay of the boss who didn't quite understand the psyche of those living in the west of Scotland; after all, he was English! There was an amazing rapport between Mr Henderson and Frank Kelly, careers officer. I learnt a lot about Glaswegian humour, wally closes, religion and class structure. Frank would jokingly, on a regular basis, tell Mr Henderson that he would have to remove his green jersey if he was planning on visiting Larkhall Careers Office. However, when I moved to Motherwell and Wishaw Careers Office, I realised that there are not many people that you come across in the workplace that do not display some sort of personality disorder.

After leaving the careers service, I became self-employed and supplied local jewellers with personalised engraved glassware. I enjoyed this work as I was able to work hours that suited me and take part in craft fairs and local exhibitions.

I returned to working in local government in 1990 and really enjoyed my work in the assessor's office, where council tax and voters roll were part of my remit. I had a lovely boss called Alan and he was so helpful and motivational. Sadly, Alan became very ill and was unable to work. When he left, the loss was felt by many within the department.

I then worked in the office at Hamilton Grammar during term time to fit in with my domestic life. Until then, I didn't realise that a school office and its staff are the "centre of the universe". Working in this environment was strange. It was as if I was cut off from the rest of the world.

I then moved to work in Glasgow as a road safety assistant. This job was amazing as every day was so different and entailed working with so many different, diverse groups across society, from nurseries and schools, to elderly forums and local exhibitions where we set up camp, so to speak, at George Square or Glasgow Green. The work was so enjoyable and rewarding and ranged from cycling proficiency tests to in-service training sessions with local teachers and working with so many outside agencies such as fire, police, ambulance, home safety officers, supermarkets, exhibition centres and more. The only thing complicated about the job was the personalities that clashed within the office. At local government reorganisation in 1996, when Strathclyde Regional Council became 12 unitary authorities, I was transferred to South Lanarkshire Council's road safety team.

In an office environment, the work can be easy and straightforward but office politics can be quite challenging and this came as a bit of a shock to me. How difficult is it to just turn up and do the job that you are paid to do without the drama of getting involved in everyone else's issues! I don't know why people find it difficult to show respect for others. No sooner had you turned your back but the knife was in. I had never experienced narcissism until I started work in the roads department. I think in my career as road safety training officer, I learned this on a first-hand basis. When management in these professions realise it's not about them, but the people they serve, it makes such a difference.

'Narcissism... is based on low self-esteem and a reliance on gaining a sense of recognition or power through dominating others.'

(Tsoknyi Rinpoche with Swanson, 2012, p.60)

When I was promoted to the post of road safety training officer in local government, I encouraged every member of my team to provide the best service based on the resources available to them. We achieved Charter Mark status for three consecutive years. I believe my school motto, "aim for the highest", never left me. The sense of sheer accomplishment in providing a first-class service to our customers felt awesome and inspiring. Receiving letters from the prime ministers of that time, to thank me for my excellence in customer service, made it all worthwhile. Charter Mark was not about ticking boxes, but actually caring about the people you serve. Work is so much more pleasurable if you truly have a passion for what you are doing. In my job as road safety training officer, I had a passion for taking a proactive approach to saving lives.

If you haven't found that job which brings you inner joy, find ways of lifting your mood throughout the day. Take time, if you can, to practise mindfulness. Stop whatever you are doing and look at a tree, the sky, flowers and mindfully appreciate that there is beauty in nature. You will not have to look far.

The Power of the Spoken and Written Word

Many sayings which are displayed in offices and workplaces can have a negative impact on the way we carry out our work, for example:

> 'Self praise is no honour.' (Unknown)

I disagree with this saying, because positive self-talk is important for our mental health and why shouldn't you give yourself a pat on the back if you have done something well and achieved a goal? In many workplaces that I have been employed, it's the only praise that you would receive. I think the saying is misleading and perhaps aimed at boastfulness.

Another saying which I found demotivating was:

> 'Better to remain silent and be thought a fool than to speak and remove all doubt.'
>
> (Abraham Lincoln, 1931)

This quote was displayed in the careers service headquarters. It really impacted on my self-worth and self-esteem. It's easy to read something, especially as it's on display every working day, and take it personally.

Keeping our mind healthy is imperative for our own resilience. Mindfulness allows us the opportunity to step out of our hectic lives and just simply notice what is going on in that old grey matter. Resting in awareness allows moments of insight and wisdom to emerge. We are unable to make wise decisions when our mind is spinning like the windmills on the wind farm in a force 9 gale.

'If you're sincere in your desire to work with others, you should expect neurotic people and be willing to work with their confusion.'

'If you're looking only for reasonable, pleasant people to help, those with a clear sense of equanimity, wisdom, and compassion, you won't find many opportunities.'

(Dzogchen Ponlop Rinpoche, 2011, p.100)

I think in a work environment, we can get caught up in office politics and so engrossed and affected by others' actions but mindfulness teaches us to step back, pause and really see the truer picture. We can spend so much time trying to change things that we know in our heart of hearts, we cannot change. If we can encourage change for the better, then this is good but we spend a lot of our time and energy on situations which we have no power to change.

'... To become more effective and productive, it is important to move on the things that we can change and let go of the struggle to change the things that we can't.'

(Sinclair and Seydel, 2013, p.5)

'Don't worry if those around you aren't doing their best. Just worry about how to make yourself worthy.'

(Thich Nhat Hanh, 2008, p.64)

Best to just do our best and realise that we are doing our best.

Activity 19 – List of Employment

Write down the jobs you have had.

Activity 20 – Life Skills Learned from Your Occupations

Write down what you learned from these jobs.

Activity 21 – Amusing Experiences from Work

Write against each one an amusing experience.

Activity 22 – Challenging People at Work

Write down the names of people who made your life difficult at work. What did the interaction with these people teach you?

Activity 23 – De-motivating Qualities

Write down what qualities they had that de-motivated you.

Activity 24 – Inspiring Colleagues at Work

Write down the names of people who inspired you at work. What did you learn from this?

Activity 25 – Inspirational Qualities

Next to their names write down what qualities they had to give you this inspiration.

Activity 26 – Positive Quotes

Look for positive quotes and sayings and display them in a prominent position at home and at work. This will help to reinforce the positive mental attitude that you are aiming to provide and inspire in yourself and others. This will help to motivate you throughout the day and lift your spirits.

Chapter 6

The Journey through
Life – Relationships

Romantic Encounters

I don't think that any relationships are straightforward and I certainly don't think that we were taught about healthy relationships at school. Although I had a few male friends at school, I only truly admired one very handsome and highly talented individual, but sadly, I was not in his league.

One guy that I fancied in my first year at high school was in the bottom class intellectually but was so handsome! My admiration for him plummeted, however, when he sent me a very inappropriate Valentine's card. I do love poetry but found his feeble attempt at rhyme did not quite match my romantic expectations and did not appeal to my sensitive and delicate nature:

> *Whisky is whisky*
> *Rum is rum*
> *Come round the side*
> *And I'll show you my bum.*

My dad did not seem very enamoured by his efforts either!

My second romantic encounter was slightly better as this guy stayed near Uncle Alex and Aunt Mary. He used to cycle up and down outside their house whenever I visited them, much to the amusement and bewilderment of Aunt Mary who kept asking me if I knew him as he only seemed to appear when I was about.

Things stepped up a level when it was discovered that my next boyfriend's mother went to Brownies with my mother. This romance was cut short when we went out on a foursome and he tried to sneak us into an X-rated film at the cinema in Wishaw.

Third year in high school and hormones in our year seemed to be spiralling out of control! A Valentine card appeared from a dark, handsome stranger stating that, "Valentine, you show promise in many fields". Due to the ambiguity implied, this effort was not well-received at home!

My next boyfriend was a bit too much on the amorous side, maybe due to him having Italian genes. I literally ran away from this extremely frisky and steamy advance.

I was then infatuated by a minister's son, but unfortunately he did not notice that I was on the planet.

One guy seemed to be totally in awe of me in fifth year, but I didn't feel the same way about him.

I was then asked out by my friend's brother, who tried to get me drunk by slipping vodka into my orange juice.

At drama group, I found I had an admirer with a great personality and sense of humour but he forgot to tell me that he was married! I think it must have slipped his mind!

Then I met my first husband at work. He was kind, considerate and patient. We got on very well and we spent a lot of time together, especially at weekends and bank holiday Mondays when we would head for Ayr, Dunure or Culzean. He was very artistic and loved to paint and engrave crystal. He loved fishing and spending time outdoors. After two years, we got engaged and I was so happy to plan our wedding and future home together.

We set up home in Larkhall where we renovated an old semi-detached cottage. We really worked well together and enjoyed seeing our project progress. My father-in-law helped with a great deal of the renovation, as he could turn his hand to any trade.

We got married in July 1981 and lived in the cottage for two years but felt obliged to move due to the interference of neighbours who insisted on keeping beehives in the back garden. The bees used to swarm and I would put a net curtain over myself when I was hanging out my washing for protection, which gained me the nickname of "Nettie".

We moved to Alloway Gardens in Hamilton and in 1987 our lovely daughter, was born. I was overjoyed at having such a beautiful, healthy baby! In 1990, we moved to a bigger house nearer the local schools. Interest rates reached a record high just after we moved and unfortunately the financial strain put immense pressure on our marriage which had slowly started to crumble. I had lots of drive and ambition to do well at work and secure a good standard of living for my family, but this was not shared by my partner. I found myself holding down four jobs in order to pay the mortgage.

Loving You

I then thought that I had met the man of my dreams. Finding someone you are attracted to in every way is quite unique – the way they look, the way they talk, mannerisms and intellect. Being near someone who lifts your heart and gives you that sense of *joie de vivre* every time you see them, makes life feel rich, invigorating and blissful. I truly believed that I had found someone that I could share the rest of my life with and subsequently wrote this poem:

Loving You

My heart is pounding when I see you,
My soul is burning like a flame,
My body trembles as you pass me,
I only wish you felt the same.

Perhaps its mere infatuation,
But that doesn't ease the pain,
Of the flooding of emotion,
At the mention of your name.

When you speak to me I'm breathless,
You make me feel so much alive,
Please now show me your affection,
On your love I know I'll thrive.

Will this dream go on forever,
And forever in my mind?
Will it burn out like a candle,
Till another love I find?

Time is passing very quickly,
But the days seem long enough,
But I know I'll wait forever,
Because you are, the one I love.

by the author

The dark, low feeling that you experience when you realise that this love is not reciprocated can feel quite damaging and it's best to move on to a place where you no longer have to torment yourself by seeing that person every day.

The Charmer

I decided just to concentrate on my daughter and my work when, out of the blue, I met a charming gentleman at work who motivated and enthused me. If you are a very trusting and gullible person like me, it's amazing how you can be easily fooled into believing everything you are told. Even if you think that you are good at acting, you should always be aware of people who really deserve a BAFTA award for their outstanding performance.

'All the world's a stage, and all the men and women merely players.' (Shakespeare, 1599, *As You Like It*, Act 2, Scene 7)

The drama unfolds. Words of warning – always look out for the charmer!

The Charmer

He preys on people who are nice,
The kind so easy to entice.
Into his spell they will be led
And every untruth that's being said
Will keep on spinning them along
They will not see his goings – on.

Just one more look into his eyes
Will then oh surely hypnotise.
Each word he speaks is so sincere
But will only lead to bitter fear.
He's using you for his esteem
And what you're thinking's just a dream.

He keeps on saying the same lines,
The ones he's used so many times.
No dress rehearsal will he need
For using you for his own greed
Of power and ego and self-love
The things that only dreams are made of.

When he's on stage, stand in the wings
And you will hear the self-same things
He pledged to you with all his heart
And of his life you'd be a part
Said to another, his next victim
(And you're not there to contradict him.)

Awake and run for your own sake
He'll break your heart, make no mistake.
Comfort yourself that in the fact
He'll meet the one who'll break his heart
By feeding words that he's been using
But this time he's the one who's losing.

His heart in two she will but sever
For as you know, nothing's forever.
The casualties along the way
Will still be suffering in dismay.
But he shall reap, what he has sown,
And the curtain falls on him 'alone'.

by the author

Forest of Love

Love has the strangest habit of emerging when you least expect it, i.e., when you are not looking for it. It is like the stereogram pictures that you stare at – you can stare and search for it presenting itself to you, and, wow, it's there, clear, real, intense. You then wonder why you didn't see it all along. It's like walking through the forest – you may not see much, but you are totally aware that the trees are not only enchanting, but robustly alive:

Forest of Love

A magical spell,
A haze of warmth,
A daze in the distance, a dove
Floating high in the clear air
Breathes the forest of love.

A natural calm,
A silent breeze,
A rustling, trembling, gleeful dance.
Whispering, quivering, secret potions
A balmy scent of love's romance.

A lover's sigh,
A breathless kiss,
Two hearts as one embraced, entwined
Deep roots that spread perpetually
Through forest, body, soul and mind.

by the author

True Love

In 1998, I met my second husband at a work night out. We shared the same outlook in life and we were both hardworking, ambitious individuals. We set up home together and enjoyed many lovely times. We both went to Paris for the first time in 1999. We toured France together and enjoyed the French cuisine and culture. After four years, we got married at Gretna Green in 2002 and experienced our first cruise together in 2006. I thought my life was perfect as I had a devoted and loving husband, good health, comfortable home and fantastic holidays! Life was ideal! How lucky was I!

However, unfortunately, interference from outside our relationship has caused a great deal of unnecessary anguish over the years. I think one of the main lessons I have learnt in life is that, in a long-term relationship, nothing runs smoothly all of the time:

True Love

As I sat alone today,
Thoughts of life without you crept.
A numbness which ran through me
As if Death himself had leapt
To end this love so perfect,

So pure and oh so deep,
The pain absorbed my being
As my body sank to sleep.

The anguish was so absolute,
Desperation ran in depths.
Confusion left me doubting
And lonely tears I wept.
Love and admiration for you
Leaving breathless tears of woe,
Not knowing of your feelings
But when on waking, so –

I saw the sun so clearly,
The answers now so plain.
Love'd been dampened by the showers
The wind and driving rain.
But true love's like the seasons
There'll be cold and calm and storm,
But then will follow sunshine
And again our love is warm.

by the author

Impermanence

I have often fantasised about falling in love and meeting my soulmate. I think as a child, I actually believed in the romantic fairy tale where my prince would appear and that life would be happy ever after. I think we have to be very careful of misleading our young people into believing that there will be a "happy ever after". Nothing lasts forever.

> *'... But pleasures are like poppies spread*
> *You seize the flower, its bloom is shed*
> *Or like the snow falls in the river*
> *A moment white, then melts forever.*
> *Or like the rainbows lovely form*
> *Evanishing amidst the storm*
> *Or like the borealis race*
> *That flit e'er you can point their place...'*
>
> (Burns, 1791)

Being aware of impermanence is one thing that you totally realise when practising mindfulness. Through my practise of mindfulness, I have realised how very precious life is. It's not that I didn't think that it wasn't precious before, it's just that mindfulness has taught me to actually be in my life, in this moment, and to totally appreciate this precious life, no matter what the circumstances.

I think that being a middle child, resented by an older sibling, made me always be looking for acceptance, approval, even love, from those I encountered in my life. This resulted in me becoming a "people pleaser", which is not a healthy way to live. Mindfulness has helped me to pause and recognise when I start to venture down the "putting everyone else first" road. My mindfulness satnav will tell me to turn around when possible. Trying to make other people happy, instead of starting with yourself, is a recipe for disaster.

'The development of wisdom requires a willingness to learn from life's lessons and to be transformed in the process.'
(Ardelt, 2004)

Activity No. 27 – Advice to you Sixteen-year-old Self about Relationships

Imagine that you are sixteen. What advice would you give your sixteen-year-old self about relationships? Write these down.

Activity No. 28 – True Love in Words

What does true love mean to you? Write down five words that, in your opinion, describe true love:-

Activity No. 29– Pitfalls in Romantic Relationships

What pitfalls have you come across in your romantic relationships in life?

Activity No. 30 – Lessons Learnt about Romantic Relationships

Have you learnt anything from your experiences? Write down in one sentence what you have learnt about romantic relationships.

Activity No. 31 – Happy Relationships

Write down five things which you have experienced that contribute to a happy and healthy relationship.

Chapter 7

The Journey through Life – Mindfulness, Trauma and Resilience

Coping with Change

Life is changing constantly. Being able to cope with change is important for our survival. Stocktaking our life helps us to appreciate what we have in this moment. Keeping a gratitude diary will help to clarify what we have and help us to prepare and adapt to the future. Self-care and self-compassion are key to nurturing our being and provides us with the strength and resilience to cope better with whatever challenges are thrown at us.

After finding mindfulness, I naively thought that life would be plain sailing. Everything would be tranquil and calm and happiness would prevail.

> *"... Meditation becomes a sanctuary that people drop into to get away from things, instead of a means to lead them into a fuller life... Such people are still deluded, just very calm in their delusion. They are calm fools."* (Rosenberg and Guy, 2004, p.50)

Betrayal

Just when I found peace and harmony in my own life, I realised that one person I had put faith, time, hope and respect in, opened a floodgate and almost drowned me in their deep, dark, deceptive and dangerous den of drudge and devastation. I had to emotionally swim for my life in order to stay afloat. Initially, I was shell-shocked and numbed by the trauma and the only way I can describe how it affected me was that I truly felt as if I was already dead. My whole being felt withered and torn. I was sick to my stomach.

Sunken Heart

The following poem denotes my feelings of betrayal and trauma:

Sunken Heart

Broken in pieces,
A heart full of woe.
How could you lie for so long when you know,
My soul is so sensitive
Feelings so deep,
Love is now dead
And is buried asleep.

In a graveyard so dark,
So desperate and lonely,
Drifting around
With no place to feel homely.
Wailing and haunting,
Floating empty on high,
Perpetually spinning
In empty dark sky.

Faster and faster,
Around and around,
In a world so unfriendly
With no feeling or sound.
The pieces still crumbling,

Into powder and crust
Will eventually settle
On earth as a dust.

Deep rolling of thunder
And lightening a-flash,
With rain pouring tears
On the powder-like ash.
Washed to the depths
All muddy and brown,
The lashings of weather
Force the heavy parts down.

Now in its deep grave
Unable to breathe,
Deeper and deeper
Beneath the roots of the trees.
No sound and no colour,
No blue and no green,
Just black with no light,
The end is now seen.

by the author

Dealing with Trauma

Ruby Wax, in her book, *Sane New World*, states that, in her opinion, mindfulness is not appropriate for severe trauma. Through my own personal experience of trauma, I totally agree with her.

> *'Learning mindfulness in the midst of a stressful and chaotic life, as Marsha Linehan says, is like trying to put up a tent in the middle of a hurricane.'* (cited by Sears, 2014, p.206)

I was left devastated by the revelations about this person. The deeper I dug, the more was revealed. To be perfectly honest, it was like bereavement to me. The wonderful person I had "known" was now "dead". The experience took me back to the death of my father. It left me with feelings of self doubt and emptiness. I was like an empty cargo vessel with nothing on board and nothing to offer anyone. Had the person I had "known" and cared for "died", or had they never existed in the first place? Had the person merely been someone I had imagined or perhaps dreamt about?

Severe trauma requires expert help and guidance. Do not be afraid to seek help from the medical profession if you do experience trauma in your life. There is absolutely no shame in this. Trauma is serious, as I believe, if left untreated, it can affect your central nervous system.

You wouldn't hesitate to seek professional treatment for a broken limb, therefore, a broken heart or mind needs urgent attention.

Mindfulness and Resilience

> 'Emotional pain, the pain in our hearts and minds, is far more widespread and just as likely to be debilitating as physical pain.' (Kabat-Zinn, 2013, p.411)

Take time to heal. Always remember that you are the important one. Nurture yourself and build yourself up to full strength bit by bit. It's almost as if, when trauma strikes, your house has been flattened and that you have to rebuild it up again, brick by brick. Be kind to yourself and spend time doing things that nurture your being. Give yourself a break and nurture your soul. Show yourself compassion and give yourself the love and understanding that you would offer to a friend who is struggling.

In my experience, the only person you can really trust is yourself; therefore, it makes sense to invest time and effort in that special person. Get to know yourself and never lose yourself in others. Losing yourself in another person can happen so easily. When it comes to your life, it is important that you are in the driver's seat. So be honest and blunt with yourself and ask yourself if you are the one driving or are you being driven. If you discover that someone else is driving your life for you, find ways of becoming the driver again. Always be true to yourself. Listen to your inner voice and notice any negative put-downs and replace them with positive, motivational and uplifting sayings that will lift your spirits.

The saying, *'No one can make you feel inferior without your consent,'* in my opinion, is false. (Eleanor Roosevelt)

What people say to us and the actions they take can have a dramatic effect on our psyche. I also disagree with the saying, *'Sticks and stones will break my bones but names will never hurt me.' (Cupples, 2009)*. Of course names hurt us! Cruel words can destroy our confidence and self worth.

Mindfulness has awakened in me a sense of increased awareness to words and actions and how they can have a profound effect on how we choose to live our lives. Mindfulness helps us to be more resilient by building up reserves of energy which we can then tap into when life becomes turbulent. It's like putting money in the bank and tapping into it when you most need it. Learning new skills and having interesting hobbies can help to keep our minds active and open to achieving new things. In order not to get into a rut, we should keep an open mind to learning and try different activities. I believe that life-long learning is vital for our mental and physical health. This stops us from getting stuck in a rut and suffering from boredom and depression. Focusing on new and motivating hobbies and pastimes helps us to be creative and find more fulfilment in our daily lives.

'... In order for us to survive in the future, we have to upgrade our minds in the same way that we keep upgrading technology.' (Wax, 2018, p.53)

Activity No. 32 – Words which Express your Feelings of Betrayal or Trauma

Write down words which express your feelings of betrayal or trauma.

Activity No. 33 – A Poem or Prose which Captures Your Feelings of Betrayal or Trauma

Write a poem or piece of prose which captures your feelings of being betrayed by someone you trusted.

Activity No. 34 – A Poem or Song which Captures Your Experience of Betrayal or Trauma

Find a poem or song which captures your feelings of betrayal.

Activity No. 35 – Taking Part in New Activities

What new activity could you partake in:-
e.g. Joining a book club, Calligraphy, Growing your own herbs, Writing Poetry, Doing a jigsaw, learning to dance, joining a choir, cycling, Swimming, joining a drama group?

Activity No. 36 – Feeling Good and Nurturing Your Soul

What makes you feel good? What nurtures your soul? This exercise is about finding balance in your life.

Draw a see-saw. At the down side of the see-saw, write down the things in life that deplete you. At the up side, write down all the things that energise you and make you feel happy. This exercise aims to help you to recognise the things that you don't enjoy doing and realise the things that you do or would like to do that nurture your soul.

For example:

Downs: Being undervalued, being undermined, selfishness, being controlled.

Ups: Compassion, self-care, walking, reading, friendship, nice clothes, colours, flowers, chocolates, weather, relaxation.

Activity No. 37 – Mountain Meditation (This Mindfulness practice can help with resilience)

- Taking up a dignified posture, sitting comfortably with the back straight
- Focus gently on your breathing
- Breathing a little deeper than normal
- Try to make the in breath the same length as the out breath
- Focusing on your breathing for the next few moments
- If your mind wanders, just recognise where it has wandered to and gently return to focusing on the breathing
- The breath flowing in and out of the body, breath after breath
- Now focusing more on the out breath and seeing if the body relaxes a little as you breathe out
- Body breathes out and relaxes, mind lets go of thinking and begins to settle

- Now let your breathing return to its natural rhythm
- Be aware of the body sitting here – strong and dignified
- Be aware of any strong sensations within the body
- Are there any subtle sensations present?
- Being aware of the ground beneath the body
- Feeling the strength of the body
- Body like a mountain
- The head stretching up to meet the sky like the peak of the mountain
- Arms like sloping sides of the mountain
- Ground stable and secure like the base of the mountain
- Body like the mountain
- Breath like the wind – flowing freely in and out of the body
- Body like the mountain – strong and dignified
- Breath like the wind – free and easy
- Mind like the sky – open and spacious
- Seeing any activity within the mind as clouds, birds, aeroplanes or insects floating across the sky
- The sky remains the same – open and spacious
- Body like the mountain, breath like the wind, mind like the sky
- And any time the mind wanders just recognise the thoughts as clouds, birds, aeroplanes or insects flying through the sky
- Returning to the strength of the mountain – strong stable and dignified
- Body like the mountain, breath like the wind, mind like the sky

Chapter 8

Mindfulness for Emotional Health – Weathering the Storm

Mindfulness and Emotions

'When we are in emotional balance, we feel alive and at ease.'(Siegel, 2011, p.27)

It is worthwhile investing time and effort in achieving as much stability as possible in our day-to-day life. In order to have emotional balance, we have to be aware of what our emotions are. Mindfulness allows us the pause in our lives to become totally conscious of what is actually going on in our minds and bodies.

'Developing skills and flexibility in facing and effectively navigating the various "weather conditions" in your life is what we mean by the art of conscious living.' (Kabat-Zinn, 2013, p.li)

Finding peace and tranquillity is paramount in order to alleviate stress, making our lives easier and healthier.

'... New research into the mind-brain-body connection has demonstrated how our internal subjective states directly shape our physiological health. The negative impact of the stress hormone cortisol on our immune system's ability to fight infection and even cancer has been established.'(Siegel, 2011, p.55)

Only you know what is truly going on in your heart and mind, therefore, it is vital that you deal with emotions as they arise in a healthy way. No one can see what you are experiencing in your life. When you are in emotional pain, you may experience all sorts of body sensations: headache, pain in the gut, heaviness at the heart. No one can see this when they look at you, therefore, you must address this inner turmoil in order to keep yourself healthy. Do you even know what emotions you are experiencing?

According to Ash Rampura, posture really affects emotions. Therefore, *'changing your emotions changes your body posture, and changing your body posture can change your emotions.'* (Cited by Wax, 2018, p.59).

So throughout the day mindfully check in with your posture. When sitting at a desk or table it is important to be aware of the way you are sitting. If you find yourself slumped over your desk, gently straighten the spine and be conscious of how this changes the way you are thinking and feeling.

When standing or walking, be aware of the ground beneath your feet and how you are moving your body. Take time to be aware of your surroundings, checking in with what you can see, hear, smell, taste and the temperature of the environment. Take any opportunity throughout your day to simply step outside. Be at one with nature, look up at the sky and look at the grass, flowers, birds and insects. Be amazed at the colours and weather.

'Remember that you are a part of the world, not apart from the world.' (Choden, 2018)

Seasonal Awakening

Take time to enjoy each season and the wonders of nature:

- Spring – new growth – buds, lambs, sunshine, blue skies, walks in the park.
- Summer – warmth and light, flowers, green trees, holidays, sunshine.

- Autumn – autumn colours, pumpkins, harvest moon.
- Winter – snow, rain, winds, frost, darkness.

Ode to autumn

You may have a favourite season. I love autumn and I love how this season is truly captured by John Keats:

'Ode to Autumn

Season of mists and mellow fruitfulness
Close bosom friend of the maturing sun
Conspiring with him how to load and bless with fruit
the vines that round the thatch eaves run.
To bend with apples the mosse'd cottage trees and fill
all fruit with ripeness to the core
To swell the gourd and plump the hazel shells with a
sweet kernel
To set budding more and still more later flowers for the
bees
Until they think warm days will never cease for summer
has oerbrimmed their clammy cells.

Who hath not seen thee oft amid thy store?
Sometimes whoever seeks abroad may find
Thee sitting careless on a granary floor,
Thy hair soft-lifted by the winnowing wind;
Or on a half-reap'd furrow sound asleep,
Drows'd with the fume of poppies, while thy hook
Spares the next swath and all its twined flowers:
And sometimes like a gleaner thou dost keep
Steady thy laden head across a brook;
Or by a cyder-press, with patient look,
Thou watchest the last oozings hours by hours.

Where are the songs of Spring? Ay, where are they?
Think not of them, thou hast thy music too,-
While barred clouds bloom the soft-dying day,
And touch the stubble-plains with rosy hue;
Then in a wailful choir the small gnats mourn
Among the river sallows, borne aloft
Or sinking as the light wind lives or dies;
And full-grown lambs loud bleat from hilly bourn;
Hedge-crickets sing; and now with treble soft
The red-breast whistles from a garden-croft;
And gathering swallows twitter in the skies.'

(Keats, 1819)

I think that we can learn a great deal from the seasons as they teach us about nature's cycles. There will be times when we rest, times when we blossom and flourish, times when the weather is harsh and cruel. Bright times, dark times and challenging times! Nature teaches us to build up reserves when the going is good so that we have the strength to cope when life is difficult.

Self Compassion

Adopting an attitude of kindness towards our survival is essential. We tend to think of being kind to ourselves as self-indulgence or self-absorption. However, the care and compassion we show to ourselves is vital for our own health, wellbeing and resilience. Nurture yourself through self-care by eating healthily, sleeping well and exercising. By doing this, as well as mindful meditation, you will see a calmer, healthier you. Building up your strength ensures that you will have the extra reserves to help you to cope when life throws us those challenges when you least expect them.

'Developing our inner compassion is like becoming our own doctors and healers.' (Gilbert and Choden, 2013, p.xix)

'The nurturing quality of self-compassion allows us to flourish, to appreciate the beauty and richness of life, even in the hard times.' (Neff, 2011, p.13)

Mindfulness allows us to pay attention to our mind and body. Not only do we become aware of our thoughts, feelings and emotions, we are made aware of where we are experiencing this in the body. For example, we can be doing our mindfulness meditation and realise that our mind has wandered off. On recognising where our mind has wandered to, we can be made aware of how this is affecting the body, perhaps tightness in the stomach, pain at the heart, tightness around the shoulders. When we realise where our mind keeps wandering off to, we can maybe begin to accept things as they are, helping us to heal – accepting and allowing the thought to be there without becoming the thought. However, when we realise that the thought is entangled with strong emotions linked to a life event, instead of reliving the entire event lock, stock and barrel, we can park it as a song, poem or story of a past life, realising that we are not alone in our experience. Others have also taken this path. Take comfort in this and continue to heal your wounds.

'... Through mental training you can alter your patterns of brain activity and the very structure of your brain in a way that will change your Emotional Style and improve your life.' (Davidson and Begley, 2012, p.11)

'... Studies have shown that mindful awareness practices can improve the immune system's responsiveness.' (Siegel, 2011, p.56)

Therefore, taking care of yourself should be your priority. This is your responsibility and cannot be delegated to someone else.

'... No one is living your life for you, and no one's care for you could or should replace the care you can give to yourself.' (Kabat-Zinn, 2013, p.7)

This is not about being selfish or self-absorbed, this is about being awake and realising what self-care you require to give yourself.

Activity 38 – Mindfulness and Emotions

- Find a quiet place and sit with dignity
- Focus on your breathing
- Try to make the in breath the same length as the out breath
- Then focus more on the out breath
- Now let go of the focus on your breathing and just be aware of your body resting on the chair, cushion or ground
- Be aware of the space surrounding your body
- Now scan your body starting at the crown of the head and move slowly right down to your toes
- What body sensations are present
- Ask yourself if there is a link between the body sensation and your emotions
- Sit with this emotion and let it know that you recognise it by giving it a name
- Now draw your emotion

Activity 39 – Recognising Good Qualities in Yourself

Think of the good qualities about yourself that you show to others and write them down.

Activity 40 – Caring for Yourself

What could you do to really care for yourself today? Try to think of a way you would show a friend that you care e.g. Make them a cup of tea or hot chocolate, smiling at them, complimenting them on the way they look. Now take time to do this for yourself.

Activity 41 – Helping Yourself

What could you do to help yourself today? Take 30 minutes to organise a cupboard or shelf to help you to stay organised in order to make life easier. Make yourself a healthy, delicious meal. Go outside and enjoy the weather.

Activity 42 – Bringing Cheer into Your Day

Tell yourself a joke. Buy yourself a little treat e.g. a flower, a cake of chocolate, a nice bookmark. Read a funny book or poem or watch a comedy film that appeals to your sense of humour.

Activity 43– Capturing the Seasons

Taking each season in turn, write down what you enjoy about each.

Activity 44 – Picturing the Seasons

Draw a picture of your favourite season.

Activity 45– Embracing the Seasons

Step outside and experience the season of this moment.

No matter what challenges life throws at us, there is always a way forward.

'... What matters is to make the best of any given situation.'
(Frankl, 2004, p.139)

Chapter 9

Mindful Living

A Mindful Home

'You should regard your home as sacred, as a golden opportunity to experience nowness. Appreciating sacredness begins very simply by taking an interest in all the details of your life.' (Chögyam Trungpa Rinpoche, 1984, p.65)

Keeping a neat and tidy place to stay can impact on your energy levels and health and wellbeing. Even if you just have a room in someone else's house, it is important to make it as welcoming and comforting to you as you possibly can. The way you organise and care for your living space is very important.

'If it is chaotic and messy, then no drala will enter that environment.' (Chögyam Trungpa Rinpoche, 1984, p.75)

'We may have many kinds of ordinary happiness in our life, but it's rare for people to be truly content if their happiness depends mostly on material things...' (Dzogchen Ponlop Rinpoche, 2011, p.60)

It is so worthwhile and rewarding to visit what material possessions we have in our home. Are we hoarding things and creating unnecessary clutter?

Visit one room at a time and mindfully look at what you have taking up valuable space in your abode. Take one item at a time and ask yourself what value it has in your life. Does it belong in this room; does it have a sentimental value? Does it make you happy when you look at it? If you don't like the item at all but it is worth a lot in monetary value perhaps you should sell it. Once you have the room looking and feeling good, take a photograph of it. When we start to practise mindfulness, we realise that it's not having material possessions that makes us happy. In fact, having too many can actually distract us from leading a fuller and more purposeful life. Having a place for everything and everything in its place can cut down on time and allow you to partake in pastimes that you enjoy. You do not have to stay in a palace to achieve a welcoming and comfortable home. Making your space work for you is key.

'An abundance of material items provides such a variety of external distractions that people lose the connection to their inner lives.' (Yongey Mingyur Rinpoche and Swanson, 2009, p.111)

What I have done with my home is to try and approach it from the outside, as an estate agent would. Keeping the outside of your property neat and tidy means that when you do return home, it's welcoming and not giving you feelings of anguish, regret or a sense of being overwhelmed by the amount of work that needs to be done.

'By regarding your home as sacred, you can enter into domestic situations with awareness and with delight rather than feeling that you are subjecting yourself to chaos.' (Chögyam Trungpa Rinpoche, 1984, p.65)

Try to make the outside of your home attractive by displaying some tubs or shrubs or flowers which are low maintenance and which bring you a sense of happiness and joy. You do not have to spend a fortune on plants. I lived next door to a couple who referred to their garden as a "friendship" garden, as all flowers and shrubs had been taken as cuttings from numerous friends' gardens over the years.

Their garden was beautiful and each plant reminded them of the individual person who donated a cutting.

Your front door should look welcoming. It's the first thing that you see when you approach your house. All your visitors will see it and even your postman's day can be brightened by your nice door with easy access to the letter box instead of having to climb over clutter in order to deliver your mail. Buy a colourful doormat which is attractive and portrays your personality. Your vestibule should seem bright and refreshing to the spirit. Display some nice prints that lift your mood and make you smile. If you have a narrow hallway or stairwell, consider hanging a large mirror to give depth, light and a sense of space. Visit each room in turn and look at each one mindfully as if seeing it for the very first time. Your home should be your sanctuary, a reflection of yourself.

'... *If you care for it with your heart and mind, then it will be a palace.*'(Chögyam Trungpa Rinpoche, 2015, p.75)

A Mindful Lounge

If you are torn between what ornaments to keep and which ones to part with, why not display them on a seasonal basis. This can provide a fresh look and feel to the room. This helps us to be grateful for what we do have and be more appreciative of our surroundings. If you decorate the walls in neutral shades and keep neutral shades on the floor, then it gives you the option of changing your colour scheme by simply changing your curtains, throws and matching scatter cushions.

Make sure your lounge is as comfortable as possible. You may experiment by moving the furniture around to give you a fresh look, or, like me, you may wish to create a seasonal look and layout. One look and layout of furniture for summer, where the seating is placed so that you can look out to the garden; and one for winter where you can make the welcoming hearth or Christmas tree your focal point.

Mindfully awaken your senses to what brings a sense of harmony and balance to your living space. Display prints, photographs, paintings of scenes that help to lift your mood and

bring a sense of happiness to you. Try to always have a vase of fresh, vibrant flowers and even when the budget doesn't allow you to buy flowers, display a few wild flowers or foliage from the garden, countryside or nearby woods which you can gather whilst out walking. If all else fails, buy some artificial flowers. It's amazing how real some of these can look.

A Mindful Kitchen

Make sure your kitchen is kept clean and functional. Don't have too much clutter as this makes cooking a chore, rather than a pleasure. If the kitchen is small and there is no space to hang prints, focus on having a nicely dressed window with attractive curtains or blind. If you do not have a window in your kitchen, display a mirror with mock curtains at the side. This will make the kitchen seem larger and reflect light in the room. Keep your kitchen in good order and try to tidy one cupboard each week, working in rotation. This will ensure that cupboards are clean and tidy and you will know what stock you have in terms of food, dishes, utensils, pots, pans and cutlery. By revisiting your kitchen cupboards on a rota basis, you will be able to work out where things are best placed to make your food preparation easier and more enjoyable.

A Mindful Bedroom

'Your bedroom and your entire house are much tidier if you put certain belongings in certain places. From that, you develop rhythm and order in your experience.' (Chögyam Trungpa Rinpoche, 2015, p.99)

A merchant's chest is a good buy, as it enables you to find a place for everything and put everything in its place. You can have separate drawers for hairbrushes, medicines, stationery, hankies, nightwear, socks, swimwear and underwear. Once organised, you will be able to tidy away items easily, as you will get to know, off by heart, what items go in which drawer. This will free up a lot of precious time looking for things or trying to keep your room tidy, allowing you to do the things you enjoy most such as walking, cycling, reading or gardening, which will enhance your physical and mental health.

It is important for our health and wellbeing to have a good night's sleep. Make sure your bed is as comfortable as possible. Your bedding should be as attractive and comforting as you can make it. Choose colours that give you a sense of tranquillity.

Change your bedding every week so that you are entering a nice clean bed. Open your windows and air the room for at least fifteen minutes each day.

Keep a diary or notebook at the side of your bed in which to record your dreams.

'The future belongs to those who believe in the beauty of their dreams.' (Eleanor Roosevelt)

Keeping a dream diary has helped me to keep track of where the mind goes to in the night. Joining a dream circle has given me the opportunity to discuss my dreams with like-minded people. Many people dismiss their dreams as gobbledygook, but writing down what my dream experiences are gives me an inner pacification. I don't think we should dismiss our dreams as they are very much part of us. We may find that we have a recurring dream like the one I had about the Forth Railway Bridge. I dreamt that I drove over the bridge in my yellow Nissan Juke. The sky was dark and the water below pitch black. The railway lines gleamed like gold, as if they had been newly polished and the moon shone brightly making them glow. I have experienced this dream several times and know that I am the driver and that I am crossing the bridge from South Queensferry to North Queensferry. Just after my first experience of driving over the bridge, I visited Melrose with a group of dance friends and imagine my surprise when I looked in the charity shop window and saw Christmas cards with beautiful graphics of the bridge and Santa flying over it with his reindeer, with the message "Santa goes Forth". I felt compelled to buy the Christmas cards and send them to friends and family as the Forth Railway Bridge has always been an important part of my life. I have many family photographs with the bridge standing proudly in the background with its beautiful, structured splendour. I remember my mother telling me that it was tradition to throw a coin into the water as you passed over the bridge.

I think we underestimate the importance of our dreams. Shakespeare, in his plays, *Hamlet*, *A Midsummer Night's Dream* and *Macbeth*, is able to conjure up the importance and strength of our dreams and denotes them in a way that play with our conscience.

'To sleep, perchance to dream…' (Shakespeare, 1599, *Hamlet*, Act 3 Scene 1)

In the Bible, Joseph was famous for the interpretation of dreams.

A Mindful Wardrobe

'… Your clothing can both ward off casualness and invite tremendous dignity.' (Chögyam Trungpa Rinpoche, 2015, p.76)

Find colours that suit you and styles that are smart and comfortable. How we dress can have a tremendous impact on our day. Wearing colours that suit your skin tone and make you feel happy and give you strength are good choices to make.

Clothes can have a huge impact on our psychological wellbeing. A splash of your favourite colour can have an effect on how you feel and act. Choose your colours carefully and wisely. I love the colour yellow, which to me denotes sunshine, brightness, warmth and happiness but this colour neither suits my skin tone or makes me feel strong. Experiment with colours and textures and find what suits you best in colour, style and comfort.

I have planned my wardrobe so that the colours start at the left-hand side on the rail and then progress across the rainbow chart in order of shades: white, beige, lilac, purple, green, blue, red, black. This way, I can see, at a glance what colours to choose from. In order that you make the best use of the clothes available to you in your wardrobe and ensure that they all get a chance to be worn, create a rail-on, rail-off method, in which an item worn and laundered moves to the extreme left of your wardrobe. If you adopt this approach, you will have a mini rainbow of your large rainbow of clothes. Don't be afraid to experiment to see what works for you.

'How you dress can actually invoke upliftedness and grace.' (Chögyam Trungpa Rinpoche, 2015, p.77)

Mindful Meal Planning

Sit down once a week and plan what meals you are going to have for the forthcoming week. Try collecting new recipes from magazines or investing in a good cookbook which will tantalise your taste buds. You may find recipes online that suit your preferences.

I have been collecting recipes for years and now have a huge box of recipe files which I have categorised into themes, i.e., chicken, beef, duck, pork, vegetarian dishes, desserts, soups and salads. Cataloguing your recipes makes it easier to find your favourite dishes or perhaps to find recipes for entertaining friends, based on the ingredients they prefer. I have many friends who are vegetarian and try to always have a vegetarian meal at least once a week to sample new recipes which I can then serve them when they come for dinner. Perhaps you can swap favourite recipes with friends and family.

Try to vary your diet to include all the vitamins and minerals to keep your body healthy. A weekly plan could look something like this:

MENU

Monday – spaghetti bolognese

Tuesday – mushroom risotto

Wednesday - steak pie, roast potatoes and mixed veg

Thursday – salmon, peas and potatoes

Friday – chicken curry with rice and naan

Saturday – pizza and chips with a side salad

Sunday – steak with peppercorn sauce, asparagus and mashed potatoes

---

Keeping a food diary as part of your journal is also a good idea, as then you can gauge if there are foods which don't agree with you or foods which you may have allergies or intolerances to.

It is great to experiment with food and to make it work for you nutritionally, economically and efficiently. If it's going to be based on time constraints during the week, due to commuting and family activities, choose wisely so that you can sit down and enjoy your meals together. It may help to batch cook at the weekend, for example, when you have more time.

Activity 46 – A Fresh Look at Your Living Space

Visit each room of your house and take photographs. Make up a folder or vision board with your photos and take cuttings from magazines of rooms that inspire you.

Activity 47 – Planned Improvements to Your Living Space

Taking each room in turn, plan any improvements which will enhance your time spent there by writing down a to-do list. Once you have finished your list, rearrange the list by putting high priorities at the top. Plan a timetable and write beside each task when this will be completed.

Activity 48 – Improving Your Living Space

Take time out of your busy schedule and improve one thing in your home each week. Remember that this is an ongoing project and not a 'fait accompli'. You may have to change your living space to accommodate life events such as children, mobility etc.

Activity 49 – Mindfulness of Colours

- What is your favourite colour?
- What is your favourite colour of clothing?
- What materials are comfortable for you?
- What clothes lift your mood?
- Which clothes suit your personality?

Once you have chosen which colours and textures work, co-ordinate your wardrobe accordingly.

Organising your wardrobe by colour can really help save time and effort every day, allowing you more precious time to spend on other things.

Activity 50– Recording Your Dreams

Set aside a small notebook beside your bed to record your dreams in. Make sure that the notebook looks attractive and inviting in order to inspire and motivate you to use it. Write down your dreams first thing in the morning. If you don't have time to write, sketch your dream before you forget. If you cannot find time to write or draw first thing in the morning, carry the book with you throughout the day and take five minutes to record your dreams.

Chapter 10

Mindfulness, Insight and Wisdom – The Journey Continues

Reflections

'Buddhist texts suggest that the untrained mind can verge on insanity because it cannot regulate its own passions and wild emotions...' (Gilbert and Choden, 2013, p.xxiii)

Mindfulness provides the space in our heads in order that we can rest in awareness. By allowing the mind to rest in awareness, insight and wisdom will emerge, helping us to clarify what we need to do to make our life more balanced. Therefore, training our mind through mindfulness is important.

I believe that the trauma I experienced in 2019 could quite easily have pushed me over the edge. On reflection, I think I could quite easily have made the same choices as my Aunt May and opted out of my life. Through my mindfulness training, however, I was able to recognise my thoughts and emotions. The trauma I was experiencing consisted of strong feelings of hatred, disappointment, repulsion and rage. Although mindfulness was not the cure for my trauma, it provided me with the clarification that I required, helping me to recognise that I really needed to seek professional help. When we experience great trauma in our lives, our entire being is affected.

If I had not decided to seek help from the experts in counselling, my life could have deteriorated beyond redemption. All those lovely times I experienced in my life would all have gone. The lovely people who have made my life so enjoyable and worth living and taught me life's values: Dad, my head teacher, Mr Scobbie, my boss, Mr Henderson and my lovely daughter, Caroline.

'Let us be grateful to the people who make us happy; they are the charming gardeners who make our souls blossom.' (Marcel Proust)

Unfortunately, the actions of a close acquaintance had tipped the see-saw in the wrong direction and brought serious heartache and negativity into my life. The person I thought I knew and could trust had disappeared forever from my life, leaving a huge trail of chaos, disbelief and confusion. Although that person had not died in a physical sense, it seemed like a bereavement that I had to grieve for.

I have worked hard to rebuild my life and enjoy the basic things that really matter, such as kindness, compassion, understanding, gratitude and appreciation of life itself: the sky, the weather, birds, animals, flowers and trees. This has brought equilibrium back into my life. If people disappoint you or upset you, turn to nature and you will not have to look too far to find beauty and energy. Simple things like looking at a flower, tree, animal, bird or the sky can uplift us to where we truly can find that inner feeling of gratitude and peace.

Mindfulness for Mental Health

Keeping our mind healthy is imperative for our own resilience.

'To focus on resilience is to acknowledge that surprises will occur that are not of your own making, that unintended consequences will always occur, that nothing stays the same, and that pleasant experiences are short lived.' (Weick and Putman, 2006, p.275-287)

Mindfulness allows us the opportunity to step out of our hectic lives and just simply notice what is going on in that old grey matter. Resting in awareness allows moments of insight and wisdom to emerge. We are unable to make wise decisions when our mind is spinning like a washing machine.

I think that our education system does not teach us the basic life skills which we all need to live as healthy a life as possible. Yes, I agree, it's great to be taught in home economics how to make an apple crumble but what happens when you reach the age of 59 and your life looks like a bowl of spaghetti?

Things are changing all the time in life. These changes may not seem totally prominent to the naked eye, but isn't it strange how you can mow the lawn one day and three days later it needs cut again or you weed the borders only to realise the weeds that you thought you had dug out have popped up from nowhere. Now you could interpret this as having to be on high alert for change happening in your life, but through your practise of mindfulness, you will benefit from a platform of stability to realise what change is happening and realise what wise efforts are required to best cope with the change.

> 'Siddhartha immediately recognised that **balance** was the crucial ingredient for so much of life as this provides the condition for something new to emerge and flourish.' (Gilbert and Choden, 2013, p.5)

It is never too late to make changes to your life. My experience has shown me that mindfulness opened up some wounds from the past but provided me with the insight and wisdom to know when professional help is required and when I can return to mindfulness, which brings me into the present moment. Through mindfulness, I realised that there is a healthy path we can all follow. There is, in fact, a way through and it does not mean a way out. There is always help when we need it most and it may not always be family or friends that we need to turn to.

Mindfulness taught me that there is no shame or embarrassment around our mental health, and that through nurturing, patience and perseverance we can heal those emotional wounds in the same way we heal a broken bone and this can take time, expert help and guidance from the professionals in their field. I only wish my beautiful aunt had discovered mindfulness and realised that there were many people to help and care. Most of all, I want her to know that I understand her suffering and I will never forget her in my heart and in my prayers. Her life was precious and has inspired me to write this book in order that, through her suffering and mine, we can save other precious lives. We are never alone. Mindfulness provides the opportunity to pause, take stock, and find the healthiest route forward, beginning with the present moment.

Mindfulness makes us realise that life is not going to run smoothly all of the time.

> *'There will always be some aspect of the full catastrophe to be faced somewhere, sometime. It is **how** you face it that matters.'*
> (Kabat-Zinn, 2013, p.507)

No matter how well you plan your life, there will always have to be diversions made due to changes in circumstances.

> *'The best laid schemes o' mice an' men gang aft a-gley.'*
> (Burns,1785)

> *'Wisdom is the art of living happily. Much of that art comes from seeing how we live unhappily.'* (Rosenberg and Guy, 2004, p.132)

Throughout this book, you have given yourself the opportunity to make sense of it all by awakening your senses to the present moment. This wonderful person that you are today is a product of your life experiences so far. By completing the activities throughout this book, you have captured wonderful memories from your childhood. You have taken the opportunity to visit your teenage years and relish in the funny stories, lessons learnt and remembered the music and fashion of your youth. By completing the tasks set at the end of each chapter, you have learned to understand what your emotions are and how you cope with grief. You can recognise the heartache you have experienced whilst capturing the fond admiration and wonderful memories of your loved ones. You have also visited the challenges in your work, life and relationships, noting what de-motivates or inspires you, providing a clearer understanding of who you actually are. Through mindful awakening of your thoughts and feelings, you understand what depletes and depresses you and what activities nurture your very soul.

We know that, through self-care, compassion and kindness, we can embrace each season with hope, gratitude and inspiration. We now know that by feathering our own nest and keeping our life as healthy and stable as possible, we can bring a sense of calm and purpose into our lives. From this point, we can move forward and enjoy this precious life that we have been given.

> *'There isn't going to be some precious future time when all the loose ends will be tied up.'* (Chödrön, 2001, p.97)

Found Not Lost

> *'Practising "one drip at a time", you'll find yourself slowly but gradually becoming free of the patterns that are the source of fatigue, disappointment, anger, and despair, and discover within yourself an unlimited source of clarity, wisdom, peace, and compassion.'* (Tsoknyi Rinpoche and Swanson, 2012, p.201)

Found Not Lost

> *I am one that lives and breathes*
> *Upon this planet, all at ease.*
> *With fate before me in my hand*
> *I love my life and understand*
> *The path before me is not paused*
> *Which I am on – found not lost.*

Lost: all of life's great complications.
Found: all my greatest expectations.
Found love, found hope, found happiness
Lost anger, rage, resentfulness.
No tears, no fears or cries of woe
Just peace, compassion, inner glow.

Strong I stand with joyful heart
Of the world I am a part
This precious life that I've been given
Each mindful moment I am living.
Grateful for the chance to shine,
To make a difference, so sublime!

by the author

'Our life is shaped by the mind; we become what we think.' (The Dhammapada)

Acknowledgements

I would like to thank all the people who have shared and continue to share this mindfulness journey with me.

I owe so much gratitude to the people who have inspired me to practise mindfulness, such as Martin Stepek, Lyndsay Lunan and all the tutors and students on the MSc in Mindfulness course at the University of Aberdeen.

Special thanks to my lovely sister, Moira D'Agostino, for her support throughout the writing of this book.

I would like to thank my kind and faithful friend, Pauline Hazelton, for always being there for me unconditionally and giving me encouragement.

I am so grateful to Aileen Murray for her patience, knowledge, wisdom and understanding.

I would also like to acknowledge my cousins, Betty Usher and Janette Moore, for their local and family knowledge.

I would also like to thank my husband, Donald, for all his IT support.

Finally, I would like to express my sincere gratitude to Grosvenor House Publishing for all their hard work and efforts in turning my words and images into a real book.

Notes

Peever – The game of Hopscotch (p.20)

Gutties – Plimsoles (p.25)

Clipe – Tell (p.28)

Wally close– Tiled entrance of a tenement building (p.47)

Drala – Energy beyond aggression (p.80)

Gang – Go (p.93)

Aft – Often (p.93)

A-gley – Askew (p.93)

Bibliography

Introduction

FROST, R., (1914). *Servant to Servants, North of Boston*. London: David Nutt.

Chapter 1

NAIRN, R., (2001). *Diamond Mind*. Boston and London: Shambhala.

GERMER, C.K., (2009). *The Mindful Path to Self-Compassion*. New York and London: The Guildford Press.

WAX, R., (2018). *How to be Human: The Manual*. London: Penguin Life.

TSOKNYI RINPOCHE and SWANSON, E., (2012). *Open Heart, Open Mind: A Guide to Inner Transformation*. London: Rider.

ROSENBERG, L. and GUY, D., (1998). *Breath by Breath: The Liberating Practice of Insight Meditation*. Boston: Shambhala Publications.

KABAT - ZINN, J., (2013). *Full Catastrophe Living*. London: Piatkus.

DZOGCHEN PONLOP RINPOCHE, (2011). *Rebel Buddha: A Guide to a Revolution of Mind*. Boston: Shambhala Publications.

Chapter 3

ALBERT, M., (1975). *Feelings.*

Chapter 4

AUDEN, W.H., (1938). *Funeral Blues.*

Chapter 5

COX, S., (2021). *Woman and Home.*

TSOKNYI RINPOCHE and SWANSON, E., (2012). *Open Heart, Open Mind: A Guide to Inner Transformation.* London: Rider.

LINCOLN, A., (1809 – 1865).Quote attributed to Abraham Lincoln.

DZOGCHEN PONLOP RINPOCHE, (2011). *Rebel Buddha: A Guide to Inner Transformation.* Boston: Shambhala Publications.

SINCLAIR, M. and SEYDEL, J., (2013). *Mindfulness for Busy People.* Harlow: Pearson Education Limited.

THICH NHAT HANH, (2008). *The Miracle of Mindfulness.* London: Rider.

Chapter 6

SHAKESPEARE, W., (1599). *As You Like It.*

BURNS, R., (1791). *Tam O'Shanter.*

ARDELT, M., (2004). Wisdom as Expert Knowledge System: A Critical Review of a Contemporary Operationalization of an Ancient Concept: *Human Development,* **47**(5), pp.257-285.

Chapter 7

ROSENBERG, L. and GUY, D., (1998). *Breath by Breath: The Liberating Practice of Insight Meditation.* Boston: Shambhala Publications.

WAX, R., (2013). *Sane New World.* London: Hodder and Stoughton.

SEARS, R., (2014). *Mindfulness: Living through Challenges and Enriching Your Life in this Moment.* Hoboken, New Jersey: John Wiley and Sons.

KABAT - ZINN, J., (2013). *Full Catastrophe Living.* London: Piatkus.

ROOSEVELT, E., (1884-1962). Quote attributed to Eleanor Roosevelt,

CUPPLES, A.J., (2009). *Tappy's Chicks: And Other Links Between Nature and Human Nature.* Montana: Kessinger Publishing.

WAX, R., (2018). *How to be Human : The Manual.* London: Penguin Life.

Chapter 8

SIEGEL, D.J., (2011). *Mindsight – The New Science of Personal Transformation.* New York: Bantam Books.

KABAT - ZINN, J., (2013). *Full Catastrophe Living.* London: Piatkus.

WAX, R., (2018). *How to be Human : The Manual.* London: Penguin Life.

CHODEN, (2018). Lecture to MSc in Mindfulness Students, University of Aberdeen (The Holy Isle).

KEATS, J., (1819). *Ode to Autumn.*

GILBERT, P. and CHODEN, (2013). *Mindful Compassion.* London: Constable and Robinson Ltd.

NEFF, K., (2011). *Self-Compassion: Stop Beating Yourself Up and Leave Insecurity Behind.* London: Hodder and Stoughton.

DAVIDSON, R.J. and BEGLEY, S., (2012). *The Emotional Life of Your Brain.* New York: Hudson Street Press.

FRANKL, V. E., (2004). *Man's Search for Meaning.* London: Rider

Chapter 9

CHÖGYAM TRUNGPA RINPOCHE, (2015). *Shambhala: The Sacred Path of the Warrior.* Boston and London: Shambhala Publications.

DZOGCHEN PONLOP RINPOCHE, (2011). *Rebel Buddha: A Guide to Inner Transformation.* Boston: Shambhala Publications.

YONGEY MINGYUR RINPOCHE and SWANSON E., (2009). *The Joy of Living.* London: Transworld Publications.

ROOSEVELT, E., (1884-1962). Quote attributed to Eleanor Roosevelt.

SHAKESPEARE, W., (1603). *Hamlet.*

Chapter 10

GILBERT, P. and CHODEN, (2013). *Mindful Compassion.* London: Constable and Robinson Ltd.

PROUST, M., (1871-1922). Quote attributed to Marcel Proust.

WEICK, K.E. and PUTMAN, T., (2006). Organising for Mindfulness Eastern Wisdom and Western Knowledge. *Journal of Management Inquiry,* **15**(3) pp.275-287.

KABAT - ZINN, J., (2013). *Full Catastrophe Living.* London: Piatkus.

BURNS, R., (1785). *To a Mouse.*

ROSENBERG, L. and GUY, D., (1998). *Breath by Breath: The Liberating Practice of Insight Meditation.* Boston: Shambhala Publications.

CHÖDRÖN, P., (2001). *Start Where You Are: A Guide to Compassionate Living.* Boston: Shambhala.

TSOKNYI RINPOCHE and SWANSON, E., (2012). *Open Heart, Open Mind: A Guide to Inner Transformation.* London: Rider.

The Dhammapada. Translated by Eknath Easwaran.Tomales, CA: Nilgiri Press 1985.

Back Cover

The Dhammapada. Translated by Eknath Easwaran.Tomales, CA: Nilgiri Press 1985.

About the Author

Eleanor Gibson MSc is a mindfulness practitioner and poet. She graduated from the University of Aberdeen with an MSc in Mindfulness in 2018.

In 2013, due to stress at work, Eleanor attended a mindfulness class at the University of the West of Scotland taught by a truly inspirational mindfulness teacher, Martin Stepek.

She has been practising mindfulness for nine years and has been running a mindfulness class at her local library for over five years, receiving positive feedback from those attending.

In October 2019, at the age of 59, Eleanor experienced severe trauma in her personal life. Her whole world, as she knew it, had been rocked, leaving her with thoughts, feelings and emotions which she struggled to process or come to terms with. Her mindfulness meditation helped her to realise that she required professional help to deal with the devastating events which had left her totally shocked and numbed. In an effort to find a way forward, Eleanor took herself on a mindful journey through her life. This led her on a mission to help others who are faced with challenging and traumatic experiences which they find difficult to cope with.

She found that practising mindfulness and following the activities included within this book led to a healthier and happier lifestyle, putting her in the driving seat of her life's journey. Her motivation is to help others achieve their full potential, where mindfulness, compassion and gratitude are central to all aspects of living because:

Every life is precious.

eleanor@writeme.com